Birthdays in the Cemetery:
A CHILDHOOD IN
WORLD WAR II MANILA

Katinka Floro Rodriguez

ALFORD MARR PRESS
Seattle, Washington

First print edition: June 2016
ISBN: 978-1-943881-01-7

Cover by Æleen Frisch
Published by Alford Marr Press
Seattle, Washington, USA
www.alfordmarr.com

Table of Contents

This memoir is dedicated to Sergio, husband and friend, lover and mentor; to my daughters, Cecilia and Katrin, for their love, understanding, and patience; to my granddaughter Diana, for her generous nature and unselfish love; to my grandson Ken, for his sweetness and affection; and to my late father, Victorino Floro, to whom I owe it all.

Maraming salamat, po, Papá.

Introduction

I started writing about my childhood in the Philippines as a way of telling my story to my American-born children and grandchildren. I wanted my children to know why and who I am. As I wrote, I found that a particular period of my life kept resurfacing in my awareness, that of the period between 1940 and the early fifties: the years of World War II, the Japanese occupation of the Philippines, and the subsequent American liberation and reconstruction of the islands.

I was six when the Japanese bombed and occupied Manila. It was not until I was 10 when the Americans recaptured the city. I saw people hit and kicked by the Japanese, witnessed houses burning, heard the shooting and cannon fire, saw airplanes dropping bombs and heard them fly overhead in droves, heard and saw the antiaircraft flak and the black cloud it left in the sky after it was fired, cheered when an Allied plane came out of the black cloud unharmed, saw large skin infections on people, witnessed people selling themselves, their children, their friends in order to survive. Collaborators, victory, dollar, open city, air raid, P-38, bombing, guerrillas, shortwave, trader, counterfeit, black market: all of these were common words in my childhood vocabulary. Names of people such as MacArthur, Roosevelt, Quezon, Hirohito and Yamashita were mentioned surreptitiously, some whispered in fear. My experiences were so altered from a "normal" childhood and so different from what my own daughters had.

As I wrote, the memoir became an obsession. I relived my childhood, some memories so vivid they resembled scenes from a movie. I cried again as I remembered my childhood feelings about my mother, who died when I was six months old. Events filled my waking and sleeping dreams. I felt compelled to write them down.

However, after watching several movies on the childhood experiences of European children during World War II, including one about Jewish boys in France and England and the very entertaining Italian film, *The Nights of San Lorenzo*, I became convinced that my story—the Filipino story of World War II—needed to be told to others besides my children.

The Holocaust has been rightly kept in our minds by the survivors of the Nazi concentration camps and the Jewish state of Israel. The horror of the atomic bombs dropped on Hiroshima and Nagasaki has been described many times in graphic detail. There have been many stories told of the suffering of innocent people of Japanese descent in the United States, falsely accused of disloyalty to their adopted country. However, I have not seen any press coverage of the Filipinos' story, nothing about the thousands who died during the Bataan Death March, nor of the Filipino civilians, soldiers, and prisoners of war who suffered and died during World War II, despite the almost fanatical loyalty many Filipinos had for the United States and the Allies.

No one speaks for the maimed, the victims killed by Japanese soldiers' brutalities during World War II. The Asian women who were forced to serve the sex needs of the Japanese soldiers are too ashamed to complain. The survivors are too few and too weak to speak up, their voices drowned by the guilt felt by Americans and the West over the dropping of the atomic bombs on Hiroshima and Nagasaki.

I do not mean to diminish the suffering of innocent Japanese civilians of that time, nor that of people of Japanese descent living in the United States, who, innocently and tragically, were forced to pay for the atrocities they neither committed nor were responsible for. However, I do not want the Filipinos to be forgotten, from my eldest brother who died in the Bataan Death March, to those of the civilian resistance in the Philippines, including my father.

We now know that over one million Filipinos were killed in the war. Two hundred thousand Filipinos enlisted voluntarily in General Douglas MacArthur's army, only to be abandoned to disease, starvation, and surrender to the Japanese. Of the seventy thousand Filipino and American prisoners of war in the Bataan Death March, as many as ten thousand died over the course of only six days, most of them Filipinos. More than a quarter of a million Filipinos spent the war years actively involved in anti-Japanese guerrilla organizations that greatly aided the American forces in retaking the Philippines.

I remember the veneration and loyalty we felt toward the Americans in those days. I grew up believing the United States to be the Promised Land, the place of dreams. The American flag was a symbol to us of all that was good. My most cherished childhood dream was to visit the United States. I would like Americans to hear the Filipino side of the World War II story and to understand what loyalty to the United States cost the Filipino people during the years of the Japanese occupation.

Looking back at my childhood years in war-torn Manila, encountering malnutrition, cruelty, violence, bombs, and death, I am amazed to have survived at all. I have my father to thank for giving his children as much love and care as he could possibly have provided. I admire his courage in the face of threats of death. His support for the guerrillas fighting against the Japanese was hidden from everyone, including his children.

Only after the American forces had landed in Lingayen, Luzon in 1944 did we become aware of his underground activities. Partisans came to our house to show proof of the Americans' arrival, long before they came to Manila. We were sworn to secrecy when we were given Hershey chocolate bars. For years, I had not eaten such exquisite chocolate that melted in your mouth. It turned out that my father had given financial and other support to the guerrillas. Had the Americans not come on that February day in 1945, my father would have been targeted for beheading by the Japanese.

Like many others who are neither rich nor famous, I encountered raised eyebrows when I told friends I was writing my autobiography. Not until I read Judith Barrington's book, *Writing the Memoir*, did I find the form and voice of my memoir. I did not want to write an autobiography; I only wanted to write about a bit of my life, my memoir. She showed me how through her book.

As I wrote and recalled those tumultuous years of my childhood, I began to understand my satisfaction with a safe and secure life in a small Midwestern university town, adored by a caring husband and loved by my children who nevertheless viewed my adult life as boring because I was just a housewife.

In this memoir, some names have been changed and/or physical traits or characteristics altered to protect people's privacy. The events and narratives are true, per my recollection.

For any enterprise such as this, one owes so much to so many. My husband Sergio read the early drafts and felt there was a story to tell. He served as an audience of one as I read every new chapter to him. His comments and insight were invaluable. Kathy Mayer and her students in our Critique class at Purdue University gave valuable suggestions and comments. My daughter Cecilia, whose writing talent I admired and envied, encouraged me at every step and worked with me for hours on each chapter. Her critical eye improved a great deal of the writing. The book you are holding in your hands owes its existence to her support, hard work, and thoughtful editing.

Certain places have made writing conducive to me: the rainy weather of Liège, Belgium gave me a head start; the noise and food of Pisa and the beauty of the Tuscan hills inspired me; and the serenity of the wooded ravines of our house on Hitching Post Road in West Lafayette, Indiana urged me to complete this memoir.

Katinka Rodriguez
Oakland, California
May 6, 2001

The Philippines

The Philippines is an island nation situated in the South Pacific, north of Indonesia and Malaysia and south of China. The archipelago comprises 7,600 islands, of which only about 2,000 are inhabited. It is home to around one hundred million people, and it has the world's fortieth largest economy.

First colonised by the Spanish in the sixteenth century, Spanish customs still influence the Philippines today. The American Admiral Dewey defeated the Spanish fleet in 1898 in the battle of Manila Bay. This event marked the end of over three hundred years of Spanish rule for the Philippines but the continuation of war on the Filipinos by a conquering army. Local patriots and heroes, such as Aguinaldo and Mabini, thought the Philippines had gained its independence from the Spaniards with the help of the Americans. Little did they realize that the Americans also had aspirations of being colonizers as well.

The Filipinos fought hard and bravely. The American forces, vastly superior, overcame the resistance. That war saw many atrocities, including torture and reprisals against whole villages whenever one American soldier lost his life, prompting many notable Americans (among them Mark Twain) to expose and protest these tactics.

What made the Americans different from the Spaniards was their educational plan for the country. After martial law was lifted in 1901, thousands of teachers arrived in the islands to teach English and educate the masses. This was different from the Spanish conquerors, who spread the king's religion of Roman Catholicism, but had prevented the masses from receiving an education.

American administration over the islands continued until the Second World War, when Japan invaded and captured the country. After the war, the Philippines was granted independence by the United States. The country's capital is Manila, located on the larger northern island of Luzon.

CHAPTER 1

Birthdays in the Cemetery

WHEN I WAS A CHILD, we always celebrated my birthday by going to the cemetery. I was born on All Saints' Day in 1935 at the Mary Johnston Hospital in Tondo, Manila. Six months later, my mother was dead, leaving four young children, Vic, four, Paking, three, Nena, two, and me, Katinka, six months. We were left in the care of my father's widowed eldest sister *Tía* Emilia, whom I called *Inay*, which is Tagalog for mother.

In the Philippines, All Saints' Day is a holiday to honor the dead. As far back as I can remember, I took part in the ritual of spending part of that day, my birthday, in the cemetery to lay flowers on my mother's grave and pray for the repose of her soul.

In the morning, *Inay* and *Tía* Sisang (another of our many aunts) and we four children walked the block and a half from our neighborhood to the *Cementerio del Norte* (North Cemetery), joining hundreds of women and children, wearing mostly black or *media luto* (black and white mourning, worn after the first year after the death). The men were usually at home, although some went to the cockfights or the races.

I remember the crunching sound of many feet wearing *bakya*, wooden sandals, on the white crushed-shell paths into the cemetery. Once we got there, *Inay* and *Tía* Sisang would sit on wooden stools under a huge old acacia tree, gossiping with the other widows from the neighboring graves. My brothers Vic and Paking and sister Nena and I ran around on the grass and played hide-and-seek behind the gravestones, calling out in subdued voices because if we shouted our *Tía* Emilia would reprimand us for not showing respect for the dead.

Manila's North Cemetery

While *Inay* laid flowers in front of her husband's grave adjoining my mother's and knelt to pray, I traced the name etched on my mother's tombstone with my fingers: "Milagros Rodriguez Floro." Unlike all the other tombstones, there was neither a cross nor an angel guarding her grave. This was because my father had bought the plot from the local Masonic Temple. He also had long ago abandoned his Catholic upbringing to become an *Aglipayan,* a member of the Philippine Independent Church.

In the afternoon, we celebrated at home by eating mango ice cream and a cake with butter icing. My favorite birthday treat was a dish made of sweetened boiled corn kernels and sticky rice, which *Tía* Sisang prepared for me. Sometimes, other cousins were invited to join and play with us. I do not remember receiving nor opening birthday presents, but during my teen years, my father always gave me money for my birthdays.

During the war, we had to stop going to the cemetery because grave robbers had started opening graves and caskets to steal gold teeth from the corpses. The adults said they did not want us children exposed to the sight and smell of open graves.

Years later, in 1997, when I visited my mother's and father's graves, I was appalled to see how crowded the cemetery had become. Where once there was open space between the tombstones and many grassy areas, there were now only inches separating my parents' graves from the next ones. There was little room to walk between the stones. I stood a long time in front of the simple white cement rectangle, where the name "Milagros Rodriguez Floro" was chiseled, listing her date of death as May 6, 1936.

CHAPTER 2
My Beginning

I WAS BORN IN MANILA IN THE PHILIPPINES IN 1935. I come from a large, close extended family headed by my father. For most of my childhood, I was raised along with seven other children: my three full siblings, three half siblings, and a nephew adopted by my father whom I treated as another brother. I saw my cousins, aunts and uncles, and other relatives on a daily basis.

In my family, infants were given a formal name at birth, typically a Spanish one. However, in everyday life, the person would be called by another name: a shortened nickname or another name entirely (often Filipino). For example, my father's name was Victorino, but his sisters and brothers called him "Bino." My aunt Josefa was "Sefa." We called my oldest brother, Victorino II, simply "Vic," while we called my second brother Francisco by the Filipino name "Paking." My official given name is Caridad, but my cousin Grading nicknamed me "Katinka" after a German princess whose photograph appeared in *Life Magazine* in the mid-1930s. That is the name I have used all my life.

My father, Victorino Floro, was born in Meycauayan, Bulacan in March 1890, not far from Manila. His father and grandfather before him had been employed as goldsmiths in the small Tagalog town. As the oldest son in a family of eight children, he was expected to follow in his father's footsteps, but his father's untimely death prevented him from being apprenticed into the jewelry-making business. His widowed mother, Agustina, a strong and determined good-looking woman, did manage to eke out a living by working as a seamstress for some of her well-to-do relatives. She had been raised in a Spanish convent where she learned exquisite embroidery work. Today, the province of Bulacan is still well known for its artisans and their fine handicraft.

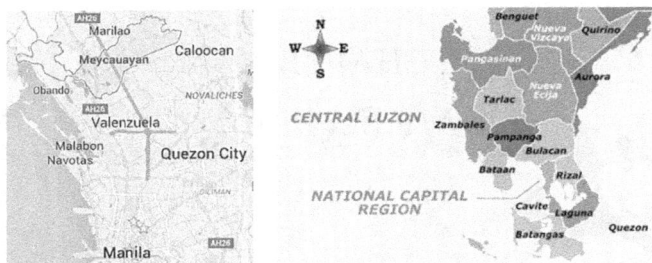

My father's birthplace in Bulacan province

My father, while still in his teens, quit school and worked at various menial jobs before the parish priest of Meycauayan hired him as an acolyte. The small salary supplemented his mother's meager income. Together, they were able to feed the rest of her family. The priests found him hardworking and eager to learn. They taught him to read and speak Spanish. Had it not been for the educational advantages the priests offered him, he would not have been able to study land surveying when they moved to Manila.

My grandmother, meanwhile, met an older man, Nazario, who fell in love with her despite her having eight children. He married her and took her and her children to Manila where he was employed as a government clerk. This gave my father the opportunity to attend a two-year program of land surveying. Agustina had a son by Nazario, Cesareo, who turned out to be a favorite of my father. His parents both died when Cesareo was still quite young, and he was raised by my father's oldest sister, Emilia.

At that time, the Americans controlled the country. The lack of English knowledge did not hamper my father much because Spanish was also widely spoken. He started out working for another surveyor. However, as soon as he had enough experience, he realized that he preferred working for himself and went off on his own.

The agriculture-based economy had started to flourish, and real estate properties began to change hands. My father saw opportunities in owning real estate. In lieu of cash payment for his services, he asked landowners to pay him with small parcels of fertile land from their vast landholdings. Many obliged. Thus began a lifetime accumulation of fertile and productive land scattered throughout the various provinces surrounding Manila. He ended up owning rice-producing fields, fruit orchards, and sugar cane fields.

In 1929, with capital from his land surveying, he started a small business to serve the engineers and architects who were busy building a larger Manila. He began the business in association with a friend, but my father later bought him out. The Manila Blue Printing Company was the first in the city to provide blue-and-white printing for architectural blueprints to the city planners and builders. The business expanded as more of its services supplied the building boom. He later also sold photostatic supplies as well as school, engineering, office, and artists' supplies.

As the oldest son in his family, my father felt it his duty to help his mother educate her sons. From his newly-acquired financial gains, my father started financing his brothers' education. He sent Martiniano, the most promising son, to the University of Illinois in Urbana, Illinois to study civil engineering. He also helped all his other younger brothers pursue their higher education in Manila, although not all succeeded. He helped his sisters financially, especially after two of them, *Tía* Emilia and *Tía* Sisang, became widowed.

My father's success in business brought him many opportunities for romantic relationships. Although short in stature, not taller than 5'4", of medium weight, light olive complexion, with a thick mustache and a winning smile, his kind demeanor and generous spirit attracted many women of varying ages whom he invited to ride around the city in his brown motorcycle with a sidecar in the late 1920s. *Tía* Emilia was very much relieved when my father gave up the motorcycle at the onset of the war. She had feared for his life and told him so.

His first liaison with Naomi, a beautiful dark woman with East Indian features, produced Hiram, my oldest brother. None of us knew much about this mysterious woman, only that she had not liked the idea of being tied down by an infant. She soon abandoned my father and their son, and Hiram was cared for by a wet nurse.

My father then met another beauty, called Carmen Katy, a Portuguese-Chinese woman from Macao. She enjoyed the wild rides on his motorcycle. I was told that she came with a circus troupe from Macao; what act she performed, I do not know. But I remember Mamá Carmen, as we called her, to be short, plump, very fair, and kind but forgetful. She had a distinct Chinese accent when speaking Tagalog. This union produced two children, Eddy and Fe. After a time, by mutual consent, they agreed to separate (due to incompatibility), and he set her up in a dressmaking business. My father received custody of the children. Now he had three of them being raised by maids, and he was single again.

Milagros Rodriguez and Victorino Floro prior to their marriage

It seemed inevitable that when my father fell in love with Milagros Rodriguez, her strict parents would object to their relationship. They were neighbors in the Binondo district of Manila. She was the neighborhood beauty, granddaughter of a Spanish captain from Madrid who came to Manila in search of fame, gold, and adventure but found instead a Filipina beauty whom he could not leave behind. At thirty-two, Milagros was just getting over a love affair that turned sour (and had produced a son). Milagros saw kindness, love, and acceptance from her new suitor, despite her family's disapproval of his purely Filipino background. My mother's family never accepted us, and we had almost no contact with any of them. Nevertheless, the union was a happy one, producing four children in five years: my brothers Vic and Paking, my sister Nena, and me. Their marriage was ended tragically by her death in 1936, only six months after my birth.

I have no memories of my mother. The only images of her I have are a few pictures taken before and after her marriage. The only picture of her with any of her children is one with my father and oldest brother, Vic, when he was a baby. She did not have time to have her picture taken with any of her younger children. Even my oldest brother Vic, who was four when she died, has only a faint memory of her.

Milagros Rodriguez

I remember using the family silver and lace-edged linens with her initials, MRF. The white linen napkins and matching table-cloths were exquisitely worked with hand embroidery that she did herself. Sheets and pillowcases that we used every day also showed her meticulous handiwork These items must have been part of her trousseau.

Sadly, I do not have any of my mother's things left. The silver flatware disappeared piece by piece during the war. My half-sister Fe had all the initials removed from my mother's linens. I felt sad at this, but, at the time, I did not have the courage to complain or even mention it to my father. The linens eventually wore out from constant use and laundering. Eventually, my older brothers and other relatives were able to salvage some of my mother's earlier pictures, and they sent me copies. These are the only treasures I have of my mother, the only mementos of her thirty-seven years of life.

I can only imagine that she must have cradled me in her arms when I was fussing, comforted me, and perhaps sang a Spanish lullaby to soothe me. I probably wore the same long lace christening dress that I saw in a photograph of Vic when he was baptized. We were all baptized as Catholics at the same church in Santa Cruz even though my father professed to being an *Aglipayan* (a member of the Philippine Independent Church). Our godparents were my mother's close friends. I lost touch with my godmother after she left for America just before the war.

I often look at my mother's pictures, frozen at a young age: a beautiful, sad-looking woman, short and thin, curly brown hair knotted at the back, doe-eyed, dressed in the latest fashion of the late twenties, looking very much like her Spanish ancestors. Her later pictures with my father and Vic showed that she had gained weight with motherhood.

I could see that I got her pointed chin, her thick hair, and perhaps her thin lips. My nose, round face, and forehead definitely are from my father's family, the Floros. My sister Nena has her eyes and her sad and faraway look, but again my father's nose. Vic resembles my mother the most; Paking, my father. Once while visiting relatives in Quezon City with my brothers, we met an old friend of my mother whom I had never seen before. She looked at me for a long time, then said, "You don't look at all like your mother. She was very pretty."

While growing up, sometimes I would pretend my mother was not dead. I imagined her just living apart from us, to return and reclaim her place later. When I was a child, I often cried when I thought about my mother while in the bathroom, the only place that I could lock and have privacy. I daydreamed about what my life would have been like had my mother lived. I imagined her to be very loving and attentive to her children. After I married and raised two daughters, I envied them, their luck at having had a mother, as I had always envied all my friends who had mothers.

Some years after my mother's death, my father became involved with a woman named Flora with whom he had three more children. She was never referred to as his wife and was considered his mistress. She did not share our family home. No one in the family liked Flora, who was suspected of seeing other men. My two brothers used to go to her house above the bowling alley owned by my uncle to throw stones at her. They called her *Buni*, a name that refers to several diseases characterized by skin rashes. After Flora died from tuberculosis, my father took pity on the three children—who for some reason he had never officially acknowledged—and sent them to live with my oldest brother, Eddy.

My father's fourth wife was Fidela, a widow with five children who had worked for him during the war. They remained together until my father's death. *Aling* Fidela conceived a child with my father, but she miscarried and had to have a hysterectomy.

My father referred to all of his partners except for Flora as his wives. We children were told that our parents had been married, and my father informed us that he had married *Aling* Fidela. They went away together on a honeymoon. But it turned out he had not officially married any of them. During my father's final illness, Fidela brought a minister to his deathbed to try to persuade him to marry her. She was unsuccessful. It seemed that he had never believed in matrimony and would not change.

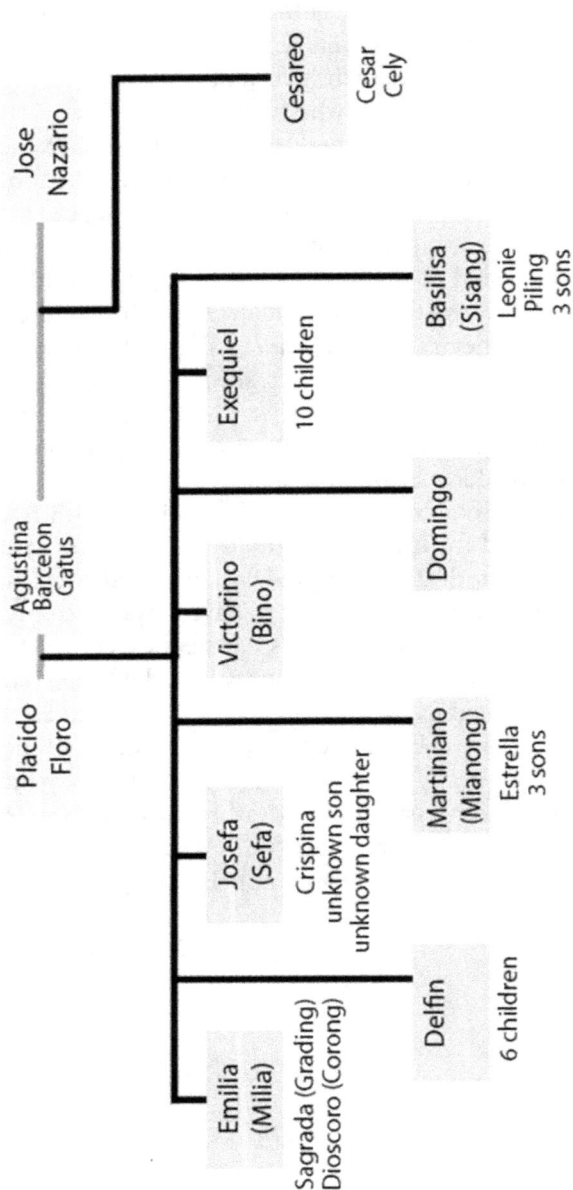

Husbands and children of Agustina Barcelon Gatus

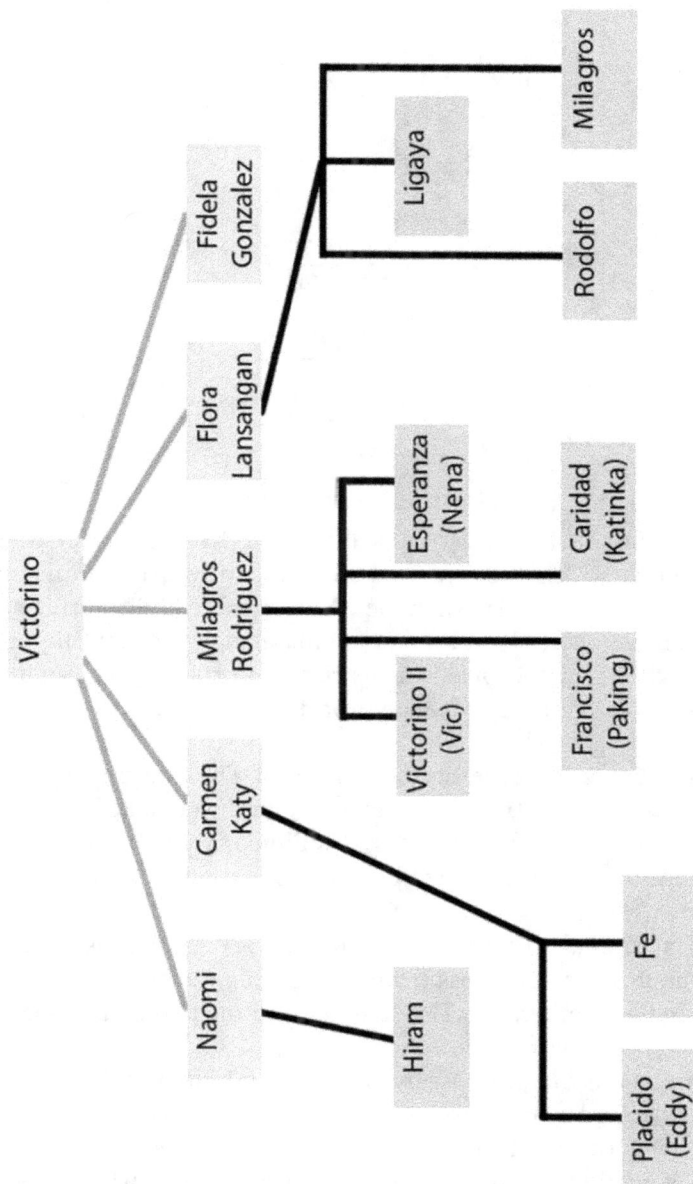

Wives and children of Victorino Gatus Floro

CHAPTER 3
Inay

NOT LONG AFTER MY MOTHER DIED IN 1936, the city of Manila decided to widen the street where my family lived. Dimasalang Street was already busy when the city decided to build a bridge over the railroad tracks and make Dimasalang into an important thoroughfare to the business district. Unfortunately, my father's house stood in the way. It was expropriated by the city to enlarge the street.

We left our house at the corner of Dimasalang Street and Washington Street (now Maceda Street) and were taken to live and be cared for by my father's sister, *Tía* Emilia. My father also needed someone to care for us as he was often gone for days while surveying in the provinces.

Tía Emilia's house was on the corner of Dimasalang and Washington streets across from my father's house. She lived next door to her brother, our *Tío* Ezequiel, and the two houses shared a common courtyard.

Inay's was a large house by Filipino standards, with three sizable bedrooms and a bathroom on the second floor. Downstairs was a large living room with a grand piano, a radio console, and a table for playing mahjongg, a spare room that my father used when he was in town to visit us (as well as a large poker table), and another bathroom.

My aunt Emilia (seated) with her daughter Grading,
her husband Patricio and her son Corong (left to right)

Because *Tía* Emilia was not a wealthy woman, my father paid for our room and board and provided financial support for the whole household. *Tía* Emilia's two children and their spouses also lived with her. My father paid for the remodeling and enlarging of my *Tía*'s house. I came to call her *Inay*, which is Tagalog for mother.

I came to *Inay*'s house when I was six months old. She was almost fifty, recently widowed with two married children. *Inay*'s daughter Grading and son-in-law Larry, their son Popoy, and *Inay*'s son Corong and his wife Nene all shared the house with her. After we came, seven adults (including *Inay*'s cook and maid) and five children lived in the house. My one-and-a-half-year-old sister Nena and I shared *Inay*'s bedroom.

Much of my day-to-day care was done not by *Inay* but by Isabel, my nursemaid. When Isabel was hired to take care of me, she was barely twenty. However, she came highly recommended as an excellent nursemaid, having taken care of her own siblings due to her mother's poor health. She was better educated than most servants, having completed high school. She was very dark, tall, not especially good-looking, but had a laugh that was repetitive, low but very contagious. I always felt reassured every time I heard that laugh and knew she was nearby.

Isabel had strong muscular arms and delighted in showing them off to me. I enjoyed feeling the tight muscles on her upper arm. She loved to lift and carry me on her hips, sometimes on her back, even when I could already walk.

Inay frequently scolded her, "You're spoiling that child! You don't need to carry her around all the time."

Isabel would smile and say respectfully that I was very light. It was true that I was very thin and sickly during the first five years of my life.

Every night at bedtime, I would beg Isabel to tell me a story. Isabel loved to tell stories about her life in Ilocos Norte. She also knew many myths and fables about the countryside that she had heard from her grandmother. Sometimes, Isabel would tell Nena and me stories of how certain mountains or rivers got their names. In a sing-song manner, she would begin, "Once upon a time, there was a pretty young woman with long hair ..." Sometimes I would fall asleep before hearing the end, so she had to repeat that story from the beginning the following night. I always tried to stay awake so that I would hear how her story ended. "And that's how Mount Makiling got its name," she would end the fable.

I always listened, enraptured by her stories. My older brothers would make fun of me for believing the stories, but I did not care if they were true or not. I just loved listening to Isabel talk.

Inay was thin, and she appeared tall to me even though she was shorter than my father's 5'4" frame. Her long, wiry salt-and-pepper hair, thinning at the ends, was pulled back and knotted at the nape of her long, graceful neck. The Floros, perhaps owing to some Chinese ancestors, were all fair complexioned compared to most Filipinos, and she was no exception. She also had all their distinguishing features: bushy eyebrows that gave the appearance of a frown, wide-set almond-shaped eyes, wide nose, small delicate mouth, and smooth skin.

Tía Emilia possessed two habits that were common to women of her age in the Philippines in the nineteen thirties and forties. She smoked cigarettes with the lighted end inside her mouth (it avoided having to puff and blow out the smoke incessantly), and she chewed a betel nut mixture that stained her teeth red. When *Inay* took the cigarette from her mouth some minutes later, it was wet, soggy, and smelly. For these reasons, *Inay* smelled not of the cologne her daughter gave her as a birthday present but of wet cigarette and betel nuts.

One hot July day in 1941 (I was about six), I heard *Inay* calling to Isabel to go to the store to buy her cigarettes. I rushed outside to accompany her. I had enough money collected from my brothers to buy a whole pack. When I got home with the cigarettes I had purchased, my brothers and I took turns puffing outside the house, hidden from the adults. We coughed a lot and ended up throwing the cigarettes out in disgust. Luckily, none of us picked up the habit of smoking even though we all tried it at a very young age.

My sister Nena and I always fought for the honor of mixing and pounding in a mortar and pestle the mixture that *Inay* chewed: a combination of green leaves, betel nut, and a chalky white substance (which I later learned was talc). Out of curiosity, I sometimes would taste the concoction before giving it to *Inay*. It was very bitter. I could never understand how she could like it. She chewed on it after a meal, making her mouth and tongue red. Sometimes, her dentures would click as she masticated the betel nut. When I asked her why she chewed it, she said that it was her *digestivo*, an aid to her digestion.

Inay loved eating salty foods, as most Filipinos did. She had to dip every dish she ate in a salted fermented fish sauce called *patis*. Everything we ate, from green mangoes and grapefruits to cooked dishes, had to be sprinkled with or dipped in *patis*. It took me a long time to get rid of this bad practice of "salting" my food with *patis*.

Even though I loved *Inay* very much, I was afraid of her. She often slapped my face, pulled my braids, or twisted my ear if I displeased her. She disciplined us for any small infraction. I kissed her only to say "good morning," "good night," and "goodbye." She never hugged me.

I felt closest to *Inay* when I massaged her scalp. She always asked me to do it after her afternoon naps. It was the only time I was able to touch her. I loved putting my fingers and hands on her tight scalp, kneading and massaging it. She looked forward to this, telling me it eased her tension and relaxed her.

After her massage, she was ready to play mahjongg with her friends who came every afternoon. Mahjongg is a Chinese game using ivory or bamboo tiles. Three or preferably four players sit around a table, each building and breaching a wall in a prescribed manner. There are four different suits; each tile in a suit is numbered one through nine. I loved watching my aunt and her friends play mahjongg. I learned to play the game at an early age, before I went to first grade.

In the evening, the noise of the mahjongg tiles was replaced by the sound of *Inay*'s voice as she prayed the novenas to the Blessed Virgin Mary. We were not obliged to pray with her as long as we remained quiet. She knelt on the cold terrazzo floor before her makeshift altar as she recited the rosary.

Every afternoon, a servant purchased from a street vendor several leis of white *sampaguita* and green *ilang-ilang* (native fragrant flowers) and draped them around the neck of the statue of the Virgin Mary, their scent permeating the room. The one-foot statue of the Virgin Mary, dressed in white with a blue sash tied around her waist, stood with outstretched arms on a dresser topped by a vine-embroidered white linen cloth.

We children were often hungry during those years, especially my brothers Vic and Paking. I remember the meals at *Inay*'s house. The children were served first, separately from the adults. A typical dinner for the four of us might consist of a single chicken breast cut into quarters, accompanied by rice (we ate rice with every meal). When we asked for seconds, we were refused. They told us, "You'll get worms if you eat too much meat" or "You'll get a stomachache if you overeat." The children also often did not get dessert since it was prepared last and was not ready by the time we had finished our meal. However, after dinner, we divided a mango five ways. Mangoes were my favorite fruit, and I never seemed to get enough of them.

This was the way we ate our mangoes. Each side of a mango was sliced, and then halved, to yield four portions. These were eaten with a spoon. The middle pit was the fifth portion. I liked the pit section because I could eat it as if I was playing a harmonica. There was still enough sweet flesh to lick and suck. But I had to be careful. In addition to the juice running down my elbows and staining my dress, my throat got itchy and scratchy if I ate too much of the fibrous part of the pit. This happened to me every time I got too enthusiastic.

The adults, consisting of my aunt, her two children and their spouses, ate afterwards. The children were scolded if we made noise during the adults' dinner or tried to enter the dining room. I remember once standing just outside the door, watching them eat their meal. They were eating *pochero* (a beef dish with potatoes, plantain, and vegetables), pork *adobo* (a stew cooked with vinegar and soy sauce), and a Spanish dessert, *leche flan* (custard with caramel sauce). Of course, they never ate any meal without rice. As they ate, a servant stood by the side of the table, waving a long fan to chase away flies.

When my father was in town, he joined them for dinner, not realizing that his children were still hungry. He was paying for our room and board, but it turned out that *Inay* was stretching that money to cover most household expenses.

My eight-year old brother Paking was brave enough, or hungry enough, to steal food from the kitchen sometimes. When I saw him eating, I would turn my right palm up like a beggar asking for food and say, "Ingge" (by which I meant "Give me!"). Paking was generous with me and often shared whatever food he could get his hands on. I remember hearing him crying once and complaining to my aunt, "Whenever I'm hungry, they tell me I can't eat before dinner time because it would spoil my appetite. But then after dinner, they tell me I can't eat because I just had a meal. But I'm still hungry!"

Sometimes when my father was in town, we would be taken to Luneta at sunset. Luneta was a park next to Intramuros and Manila Bay with wide lawns and shady acacia and flame trees. We would watch the most glorious colors painted by the setting sun over Manila Bay as we enjoyed the cool breezes. I still have a special place in my heart for Manila Bay. My longing to go abroad must have started there as I watched ships of different countries pass by before they set anchor at the port of Manila. My first sight of a fireworks display came on our Independence Day at Manila Bay. That was a very exciting time for me.

Ambulant vendors tempted us with boiled peanuts, sweets, and *balut*, cooked duck eggs with embryos inside. My father didn't want us buying from the food vendors when he took us to Luneta, not for the same reason *Inay* gave (that it would spoil our appetite), but because he disliked children eating inside the car. He thought we made too much of a mess. He couldn't stand peanut shells stuck in between the upholstery of the car and melted ice cream staining the car seats.

Occasionally, I did get to eat *balut,* outside the car, of course. It took a special technique to eat this delicacy without gagging because of the presence of the duck embryo inside. First, I broke the shell and sucked the salty juice without looking at it. Then I swallowed the whole egg in its entirety. What I did not want to do was to examine it closely before eating because of the ugly appearance of the semi-fertilized, hairy embryo. I also avoided biting into the duck's embryo itself so as not to taste the body parts. Once in a while, I would forget and then tiny bits of hairy legs would get stuck in between my teeth. Yuck! But it was very delicious, and everyone said it was nutritious. I loved it.

We suffered often from colds and viral infections when we lived in *Inay*'s house. We were all very thin, and we often had open sores on our legs. *Inay* attributed illnesses to cold and dampness. She thought we would catch cold from the late afternoon dew if we played outdoors after five o'clock. We, therefore, were not allowed to go outside then. This restriction created havoc inside the house. My cousin Grading often complained of the noise we made. *Inay* would slap us across the face and call us bad children. I was most afraid of her then.

Inay sometimes told me that she suffered from a bad heart. I used to be frightened that she would die and leave us orphans again. Even though she did not treat me well, she was the only mother figure I knew.

CHAPTER 4

The Courtyard

THE SHARED COURTYARD WAS THE CENTER OF ACTIVITY at *Tía* Emilia's and *Tío* Exequiel's adjacent houses. I spent many hours playing there and watching all the different people who worked and came to visit. Sometimes I woke at dawn, entered the courtyard before anyone else, and saw the morning sun break through wispy clouds.

Early in the morning, Juana, our laundress, a small, dark woman in her fifties, entered the courtyard to begin her daily ritual of washing that day's dirty clothes. She smoked continuously in the same manner as Inay, placing the lighted end of the cigarette inside her mouth. She had a valid reason for not taking the cigarette from her mouth: her hands were just too wet and too busy. She washed clothes while seated on a small bench with short legs. She tucked her legs under her black skirt, stooped over a large circular corrugated iron tub, like the plastic swimming pools of today's children. She scrubbed the clothes with her two hands, sometimes beating stubborn stains with a piece of wood, soaped them, rinsed them in clear water several times, and hung them up to dry.

Juana strung up ropes made from Manila hemp across the courtyard, from the iron bars of the lower windows of *Tío* Exequiel's house to the papaya tree and back. Starched white sheets straight and hard as cardboard, children's faded play clothes, women's multicolored print dresses, and assorted household linens and cotton towels vied for space under the sun and enjoyed the tropical breeze from the distant ocean.

The clothes did not take long to dry due to the brisk wind and hot sun. Then Juana removed and stored the clothespins in a special white cotton bag, gently folded the clothes into her rattan basket, and untied the clothesline, neatly rolled it, making it ready for the next day's wash. She sprinkled water on the starched clothes and ironed them as they were dry. It took her about four hours of straight ironing. The laundry was her only duty, but it was back-breaking work since she washed clothes for about fourteen people, perhaps more. And she had to do it every day.

Perspiration dripped down her neck as she replenished the hot charcoal inside her heavy iron a number of times. Like a concert pianist who rested her hands and went through rituals to save her hands, our washerwoman rested her hands on the table for half an hour after ironing, without allowing water to touch them. She believed that washing her hands after ironing would give her rheumatism. Then her day was done.

Rain or shine, the fruit and vegetable vendor arrived soon after daybreak, riding a cart pulled by a *carabao*, water buffalo. His little boy sat astride the *carabao's* bony back, barefooted and wearing shorts and a torn shirt, a small *salakot* (native hat) on his head. He never uttered a word to me. I would look at this silent rider, envious of his seat on the *carabao*. Unlike horses, which scared me because of their agility and high spirits, a *carabao* moved so slowly, seemingly waiting for the gentle coaxing of his master to go forward. It showed no temper. I longed to exchange places with that little boy, but my timidity prevented me from asking.

The old man and Inay would always haggle over price and quality of the merchandise. The fruits and vegetables were sold by the dozen or by the unit. Sometimes, the old man would split open a fresh *santol*, a native fruit similar to a nectarine, to show its ripe juicy flesh. He would give me half, and his young son would eat the other half. That was the only time I would see a smile come out of the boy's face, mirrored on my own. After tasting the sweet, juicy fruit, I would implore my aunt to buy some.

The "Egg Lady" also came every day before lunch, pushing a small cart filled with eggs protected by hay. She wore a long black dress, her gray hair braided and covered by a red paisley cotton bandanna. Shoes cut up in front revealed dirty toenails. She brought her eggs in a woven basket into the kitchen. We scanned each egg in front of a lighted candle or sometimes placed them in a basin of cold water to determine freshness.

"This egg floated, *Aling* Lulay. It's not fresh. Give me another one," Inay would say as she rejected the brown egg I had just placed inside the basin.

"These eggs are fresh, señora. I picked them up myself from the coop in my back yard. See, touch them. They are still warm."

"You know I don't buy eggs that are not fresh. Please give me another."

"The señora is very particular. But since you are my best customer, you get to pick the best eggs."

Every day, Inay purchased two dozen brown eggs from her. I loved touching the smooth and fragile shells of the eggs, taking great care in placing them in the basin of water. When we were fortunate, we sometimes received a soft-boiled egg for breakfast.

The ice man came in the afternoon to deliver a big block of ice for our icebox. Electric-run refrigerators were either too expensive, too new, or just had not come to our part of Manila. The young man came in a horse-drawn enclosed van with the word in capital letters HIELO (ice) written on both sides. The van contained huge blocks of ice that the young shirtless man delivered house to house in our neighborhood. We would stop our play, watch him spear a large block of ice with his giant metal tongs and carry it atop his broad shoulders, dripping icy water on his burlap-draped shoulder. Sometimes, we would sneak up to his van to touch the wet, smooth surface of the ice blocks, cooling our warm hands and bodies. The ice kept our icebox cold, preserving meat and cooked dishes and cooling our fruit drinks.

The ringing of a bell, similar to my kindergarten teacher's, awakened me from my nap to catch the popsicle man. A barefooted young man pushed a two-wheeled cart with ice-enclosed compartments, painted on both sides with pictures of bright orange and chocolate popsicles, melting on a stick. For five centavos, I could buy a single orange popsicle, wrapped in paper and held on a stick like a tongue depressor. Twin popsicles cost ten centavos. It was not practical to buy twin popsicles unless you shared with someone. They were quick to melt under the blazing sun. Popsicles were a soothing treat on a hot afternoon. I always looked forward to hearing the popsicle man's bell.

Once a month, very regularly, an old man of around fifty-five, barefooted, with sun-drenched skin and closely cropped gray hair, wearing faded knee-length khaki shorts and a much-darned polo shirt, would arrive in our courtyard pushing a wooden box-like cart with two large-spoked wheels. The singsong lilt of his voice and the creaking of his wheels announced to us children that *Tío* Milio had arrived. He had become known around Manila as he wheeled his cart, sharpened knives for people, and discussed religion with them. He also enjoyed talking about politics. We often saw him around the city surrounded by a curious crowd, talking religion and politics. We dubbed him "The Philosopher." When he arrived, we stopped whatever games we were playing to watch him pedal by foot his various round flat stones and see the sparks fly from the knives and scissors he was sharpening.

Tío Milio (short for Emilio) was a second cousin of my father on his mother's side. His only source of income came from his knife-sharpening business. Sometimes my father gave him extra money when he came into the house, and, at my father's invitation, he occasionally joined us for lunch. He had a wife who did laundry for other people, and seven children, mostly girls. One of the girls worked for us as a maid for a year.

Tío Milio loved to argue religion with anyone. He belonged to a very small minority sect, the Jehovah's Witnesses. At that time, the Philippines was about 98% Roman Catholic, so *Tío* Milio had lots of people with whom he could argue. He was never angry or rude; he always spoke with a smile on his face, showing a toothless grin. He poked fun at the Catholics' worship of one God alongside the presence of so many saints and idols in church. He especially liked to discuss religion with youngsters because they could not defend their religion successfully. He loved to provoke my brothers. Nobody won or lost in these discussions, but *Tío* Milio always came out of it feeling victorious and elated.

Another man who visited regularly with merchandise to sell was the Sikh. He sported a long gray beard that reached down his chest, was dressed in something that I thought looked like white pajamas, and wore a white turban wound around his head. He carried his treasures in a white bundle: the most gorgeous linen tablecloths hand-embroidered in China, matching table napkins, sheets and pillowcases, all embroidered with multi-colored threads, silk pajamas in vivid red, and silk brocade slippers from Hong Kong. His bundle smelled of the sandalwood fans he brought for sale. My aunt bought the sandalwood fans we took to church from him.

One day, after he had opened his bundle, Nena and I crowded closer than usual, savoring the fragrant sandalwood as he untied it. Another time, I was called to try on a pair of the red silk brocade slippers. The padded slippers were embroidered with black dragons and white vines with small flowers. They were soft and gentle, like a baby's skin. It felt like walking on clouds when I wore them. I was proud of my padded red brocade slippers, which I used only inside the house.

After lunch and siesta, the courtyard became the domain of the children. Because we played ball and other running games, dug holes for our game of marbles, and cooked on our miniature pots inside the courtyard, no plants would grow on it, except for a solitary male papaya tree that produced no fruit but provided us with a lacy kind of shade at noon. A few sturdy bushes that bore no flowers, but were strong enough to accept abuse from many active children, grew around its borders. A maid watered the bushes every morning and dampened the soil to contain the dust that got into our hair, clothing, and shoes.

One day, while Nena and I were cooking rice in our toy pot over the miniature earthen stove in the courtyard, my brother Vic sneaked up behind us and threw something into our pot.

"What did you put in our pot?" asked Nena.

"Yikes! It's moving!" I shouted.

"Oh, it's just a frog. Your rice dish should be tastier now."

"We are not eating a frog. Get it out of there!" Nena ran inside the house to get our *Tía* Emilia.

"Inay, look what Vic did. He threw a frog into our rice pot. It's so filthy. Now we can't eat the rice anymore," Nena complained to my aunt, crying.

"Victorino," my aunt said, "how many times have I told you not to bother your sisters. Now you have spoiled a perfectly good pot of rice. Go inside this minute, and I'll deal with you later."

We both stuck out our tongues at Vic. We knew he would be spanked.

We sometimes ventured outside the courtyard and explored the nearby neighborhood. I remember when the Dimasalang railroad bridge was under construction. I was allowed to go as far as the foot of the bridge, riding my new tricycle in the company of Isabel. While on a ride one afternoon, I saw a dog being chased by several men and children with sticks. Isabel, frightened at the sight of the mad brown dog with saliva frothing out of its mouth, turned my trike around and pulled me down the bridge as quickly as she could, saying, "We need to get out of here, Katinka. That dog has rabies!" I heard later that the dog had run in circles trying to escape its pursuers, and was finally cornered at the top of the bridge where it had jumped to its death.

Everyone was terrified of rabies. We were often admonished to never approach any strange dog. We heard many stories of people who had been bitten by dogs that turned out to be rabid. A popular actor had recently been accidentally bitten by a fan's dog. He ignored the advice of his own physician to have anti-rabies shots and died as a result. His funeral cortege passed in front of our house on its way to the *Cementerio del Norte*. An endless procession of cars carried multicolored floral wreaths in all sizes, bringing the lingering smell of the *azucenas*, white lilies, as the cars passed by. Women in black, riding inside black limousines, wiped their tears with white handkerchiefs. Thousands of fans of all ages mourned the actor's death. They wept loudly and unashamedly as his funeral cortege passed; some even fainted at his funeral. He had appeared in many movies where he was the invincible hero; now he was gone.

Living on Dimasalang Street, we saw funerals pass by almost every afternoon. You could tell the importance and wealth of the deceased by counting the cars in the cortege and the number of wreaths. We would stop playing on the sidewalk whenever we heard a hearse playing "Ave Maria" coming up the street. We would watch the procession, and the adults told us to always make the sign of the cross as they passed by. The poor could not afford a hearse, so they would just carry the coffin, often white for a child. They would walk by in silence.

Although we didn't know it at the time, watching funerals in the summer and fall of 1941 was only a small taste of the death and destruction that we would witness in the near future.

CHAPTER 5

December 8, 1941: The Bomb

THE DRONE OF MANY PLANES FLYING OVERHEAD followed by the whine of the city sirens woke me from my afternoon nap. I jumped, almost falling out of my narrow bed, and pushed aside the tied mosquito net. My brother and sister were already poking their heads out of the window. Before I could join them, I heard a loud "Boom, boom, boom!" followed by an earth-jarring bang that rattled the windows and shook the cold terrazzo floor I was standing on. I heard screams and shrieks from the women in the house, and someone began to pray, "Santa María, Madre de Dios..." (Holy Mary, Mother of God).

"That sounded like a bomb," my father said, awakened from his nap on the living room rocking chair. "It must have fallen nearby."

"Papá, I can see smoke from my bedroom window," my nine-year-old brother Vic called.

My father and his brothers had been glued to the radio earlier that day, listening to the news about the unprovoked attack. The much-talked-about War had begun. It was December 8, 1941, a religious holiday in the Philippines (the Feast of the Immaculate Conception). Only yesterday, Japan had attacked Pearl Harbor in Hawaii, which in my youthful ignorance (I was six) I had mistakenly placed somewhere in the Philippines. Since Manila was called "the Pearl of the Orient," I had assumed anything called "Pearl" belonged to the Philippines.

No one, not even General Douglas MacArthur, had thought the Philippines would be the next target of the Japanese. News from the radio reported that the American planes, like in Hawaii, were caught parked wingtip to wingtip on their Filipino bases and were destroyed before they could get airborne to mount a defense.

Ignoring my father's warning to stay indoors, the other children and I sneaked out of the house. I ran after my older brothers and sisters. It was a beautiful day in December, sunny, warm, and dry. My feet dragged in the dust because my red brocade slippers kept slipping off as I ran. I knew I might be spanked later for my disobedience, but I did not stop. Children in various states of dress and undress followed us.

The neighborhood men, all home from work due to the holiday, awakened from their midday siestas, were also running towards the end of the block, where a wisp of dark smoke and swirling dust marked the area where the bomb had dropped. The women of our neighborhood in the Santa Cruz district of Manila stayed at home, praying, and peeking from the iron-barred windows. In the Philippines, it was considered immodest for women to go running out into the street. They would get their news of the incident later from their children and husbands.

As I approached the gathering crowd, I could only see backs and feet of men and children. A strong, strange smell overpowered me. It was of burning banana leaves, reminding me of the picnics we had at *Tía* Edeng's house in Meycauayan, Bulacan, my father's hometown. We had eaten rice and *lechon* (roast pork) with our hands, not on plates, but on banana leaves that had been passed over an open flame.

The bomb had fallen on an empty lot. It had missed a house by a few hundred feet, so no one had been killed. The bomb formed a small crater. I had imagined the hole would be as large as a house, but I was disappointed to find it only the size of a couple of *carabao* (water buffalo). The edges of the round hole were cut as if someone had worked his way neatly around it with a spade. It looked deep. The bomb had fallen amid blooming red *gumamelas*, hibiscus, and bent banana plants, loaded with fruits and almost touching the ground. The blast had seared the banana plants, accounting for the smell. Some of the burnt trees resembled crosses in a cemetery. After seeing that nobody had been killed, the hole lost its fascination for me, and I started to listen to the conversations around me.

An old man wearing a *barong Tagalog* (native shirt) said authoritatively, "These Japanese pilots are not very accurate. This bomb must have been meant for the Dimasalang Bridge."

"Why would anyone want to bomb that bridge? It's only an overpass over railroad tracks, not a river," asked another man, much younger, wearing a *salakot*, a cone-shaped hat made of dried thatch leaves. At that time, the only men who wore *salakot* were either from the provinces or performed manual labor. From his accent speaking Tagalog, I could tell he was from Manila.

"Don't you see? This bridge looks important from the air," answered the old man in the *barong Tagalog*.

"How could the pilot miscalculate his distance so much?" asked the younger man.

The old man answered with the confidence of an educated man. "It's a matter of trajectory. The pilot should have dropped his bomb before his target, not on his target. Then he would not have missed it."

"I'm glad that Japanese pilot missed. Think of the lives he would have taken. Thanks be to God." The man with the *salakot* made the sign of the cross. The Dimasalang Bridge, which had been completed not that long before, was spared by the bomb. In fact, it remained intact and survived the war.

I got bored listening to the two men discussing "trajectory," a word I did not understand then, and started looking around. I glanced up at the people looking down from their windows at the hole made by the bomb and recognized the three *bailarinas*, dance hall girls, who always passed by our house every afternoon, on their way to work.

"So that's where they live," I said to myself.

The *bailarinas* must have also been awakened from their naps since they were in their sleeping clothes. They became the attracttion as much as the crater. The three young women leaned out from their open window, talking animatedly and exposing their flowery silk kimono-clad bodies from the waist up. Their heavily made-up faces contrasted with the other women peering out of a different window, dark and old, wearing no make-up.

These young women worked in a cabaret in La Loma, just outside of North Manila, where men paid to dance with them. Every afternoon, they teetered on black high-heeled sandals as they passed by our house on their way to the dance hall. Their dresses were tinted with the colors of the parrot my aunt kept as a pet: red, green, and yellow. In addition to their brightly colored outfits, the women painted their faces, lips, and long nails red, circled their eyes in black, and adorned their long flowing hair with whatever flower was in season, usually a red or yellow hibiscus.

They were very young women, probably newly arrived from the provinces. Many young girls came to Manila to seek their fortune. Some came to work as servants for families like ours; others ended up working in dance halls like these women. Isabel once told me that she thought she recognized one of the women as having come from a neighboring town in her province.

"I am sure her father doesn't know what she's doing here in Manila," she said, "but I certainly would not want to be the one to tell." Isabel had been braiding my hair. She looked into the distance and frowned.

The dance hall girls passed by our house every day, even on Sundays. If we were outside playing *piko*, hopscotch, on the sidewalk, we would stop as soon as we noticed them. Although we stared in fascination at the way they were dressed, we did not tease them, unlike many of the other neighborhood children. They would smile at us and give me a pat on the head as they walked by. Sometimes one of them would ask me how old I was or would mention that we reminded them of their brother or sister back home.

But my aunt and cousins were not pleased when the *bailarinas* spoke to us. Without any explanation, they warned us not to talk to "those women."

The hole made by the bomb remained there throughout the war. It collected water from the monsoon rains and became a swimming hole for the neighborhood kids. More banana plants grew around it. I never got near it again because I was forbidden to go near the area. After the war, a yellow Caterpillar, the first earth-moving equipment I had ever seen, covered the hole, which had become a breeding place for mosquitoes. A house was eventually built on the bomb site for a new family from the provinces who did not know of its history. Their son, David, was in my second-grade class at the Dr. Alejandro Albert Elementary School. But the memory of the bomb will be with me forever.

The bomb remained a topic of conversation among the adults. This was not really anything new. They had been discussing the possibility of a war coming for a long time. It made a big impression on me when the adults had talked of going underground in a shelter in case of war. The Tagalog word for shelter is *lungga*, which also means an animal den. When I heard that we might live in a *lungga*, I couldn't imagine how we would all fit in an animal's lair. I had only seen a few holes dug up by very small animals, having lived in the city all my six years. After the bomb, I continued to listen with interest when they discussed what might happen next and what the family might have to do.

CHAPTER 6

My Family Flees Manila

V ERY LATE ONE NIGHT, I AWOKE SUDDENLY when someone raised the mosquito netting and placed a cold hand on me. It was Isabel, shaking and mumbling. "I was told to dress you for the trip to Bagbag," said Isabel, tugging on my arm.

"Do I have to? It's still dark and cold. I want to go back to sleep."

"You have to go to Bagbag. If you don't hurry, you'll be left behind, and the Japanese will get you," she warned.

"No," I cried, terrified. "Okay, okay. I'm getting up."

"Why do we have to go at night?" my sister Nena asked.

"So the Japanese planes will not see us. They don't fly at night," my brother Paking answered.

"Are the children ready, Isabel?" my *Tía* Emilia asked. "Take them to the car. Lock up the house, and follow us in the *carretela* (a horse-drawn wagon). The others should have arrived in Bagbag by now."

"Yes, señora." Isabel grabbed hold of my hand and led the four of us to the waiting car in the courtyard. We piled into the back, the older children claiming the window seats.

Pale twin round headlights illuminated the unpaved, dusty road to Bagbag. We made the drive there in a caravan of several cars and carts: my father and his seven children, *Tía* Emilia and her son and two married daughters with their husbands and children. Our trip in the dark was slow. There was no moon, and only a few stars twinkled above us. The sound of our engine reverberated through the rice fields and palm trees. It was lucky we were the only cars on the road, or we would have eaten all the dust of the other vehicles. Soon I fell asleep again.

After we had driven for a while, Paking shouted, waking me up. He pointed toward the back of the car.

"Look behind us!"

Behind us, I saw streaks of red in the sky like watercolor splashed on white paper. It was Manila burning. It appeared as if the whole city was in flames. I imagined I could feel the heat. The cool bay breeze had evaporated, leaving only the smell of burning timber. I heard crackling noises from the houses being swallowed by the flames. I cried at the thought of our house on fire. I had visions of losing everything: my toys, my clothes, our house. I cried until we reached Bagbag.

Bombing during the Japanese invasion of Manila

Bagbag was cool and dark. I cuddled next to Nena and clasped her hands tightly, frightened by the unfamiliarity with the place and the strange rural nocturnal noises we heard. I felt better when I heard some familiar sounds: dogs barking, crickets chirping, and frogs croaking. Some of the servants, who had arrived earlier in several horse-drawn carts filled with boxes of kitchen stuff and clothes bundled in sheets, had already prepared our sleeping accommodations by candlelight.

My siblings and I were assigned to sleep on the living room floor of the caretaker's cottage, a hut made of *nipa*, thatch. The windows of the *nipa* hut, propped open by small sections of cut-up bamboo, were covered with black cloth to prevent Japanese planes from spotting us, had they flown that night. Candles on tabletops, placed by the servants to light our way and prevent us from being afraid, reminded me of Christmas. The previous Christmas, my father had taken us to a celebration at the Masonic Temple in Manila (my father was a Mason). I saw for the first time a Christmas tree decorated with small multicolored lights, silver tinsel, and toys. It was also my first encounter with Santa Claus. We did not suspect that this party, where an old perspiring Santa Claus in a faded red suit and shredding cotton beard handed out plastic toys made in Japan, would be our last joyous Christmas gathering in a long time.

We did not have beds in the cottage. I slept on a *tatami* mat rolled out on the bamboo floor. It felt like sleeping on several rolling pins, but I was too tired to let it bother me. I slept soundly until the roosters' crowing woke me up at dawn. Then I remembered the bomb that fell near our house, the fires of Manila, and that this was not home.

The town of Bagbag is in an area known as Novaliches. Bagbag is now part of Metro Manila, but at the onset of World War II, it seemed very remote from Manila and safe from the war. My father had acquired a few hectares of land with fruit trees and an old *nipa* hut on it. He had been surveying farmland for a number of years, and the Bagbag land had been the payment for one of his jobs. At one time, he intended for his children to all live with him there, so he had moved his city house from Dimasalang Street by cart after the government had expropriated its lot for the Dimasalang bridge project. That house now sat on cement blocks, elevated to two stories, in a corner of the property. Four families, consisting of seven adults, nine children, two chauffeurs, and five servants, occupied the two dwellings in Bagbag: the old caretaker's hut and our transplanted house. There was no electricity or running water. A balking generator, brought from the city, provided on-and-off power.

The route to Bagbag

My first morning in Bagbag, several roosters crowing in concert awakened me. I was lying on a tatami mat next to my sister Nena, who was quietly snoring, a white cotton sheet covering our thin legs. It was cool but not cold, but I was shivering, and my teeth were chattering. I pulled my covers up to my neck. Where was I? At least Nena was with me.

I turned to my right and looked at the pencil-thin light coming from a small window, still covered by a black cloth. The darkness and unfamiliar surroundings frightened me. It took me a while to figure out where I was. At last I remembered. We had escaped from Manila, from the Japanese, to come to Bagbag the night before.

Isabel's voice jarred me from my reverie. She had entered the room without making a sound. She shook my arm.

"Katinka, didn't you want to come with me to the hen coop to pick up some eggs? You asked me to wake you up and show you where we get our eggs. Come along. I'll help you dress."

"Shouldn't we wake up Nena?"

"No need to. Let her sleep. You were most eager to get the eggs. You told me yesterday, no matter what happens, to wake you up. Come on. Put on your *bakya* (wooden shoes), and wear this sweater. It's chilly outside."

"It's still so dark. Why don't you turn on the light?"

"You don't remember from last night, do you? There's no electricity in Bagbag. From now on, you'll have to get used to candles at night," Isabel said with a smile.

"I dreamed that Manila was on fire and we were running away from it," I said.

"That was no dream. That was for real. Don't you remember we came here last night to escape the bombing? Anyway, we're safe and far from the bombs now."

Isabel had the knack of getting me dressed very quickly. She had been doing this since my mother died when I was a baby. She guided me out of the dark into another room that had an open window. The light of dawn filtered through the black curtain, and I saw a small door to the outside, leading down some steps.

"Watch your step. These bamboo poles can be slippery. Hold on to me," Isabel said as I slowly took the bamboo steps one at a time. The steps were open to the back and quite steep. I was afraid I would fall.

"Why do we have to get the eggs when it's still dark?" I asked.

"You ask too many questions. We want to get the eggs while the hens are asleep."

We walked down a pathway caked with dried mud. My wooden shoes passed over soft and hard compact ground. Tall grasses and branches from low bushes brushed against my legs. I smelled chicken droppings before I heard the cackling. Then in the dim light I saw the silhouette of a low building made of galvanized iron, wood, and metallic screen. The noise and smell became overpowering as Isabel opened a small low door.

"It doesn't smell good in here," I said.

"Shoo! Don't complain too much. Here. Put your hand here, and gently pick up an egg." She placed my hand under a feathery ball that moved and made a sound.

"I got an egg! It's still warm. Wow! I can feel many eggs down here." I got excited.

"Shhh. Don't wake up the rest of the hens. Grab another egg. Place it gently in my basket. Be careful not to drop any."

"This is fun. Nena will be jealous we didn't wake her up."

"She'll get her turn tomorrow. Come along now. We probably have enough for breakfast today," Isabel said as she closed the door to the coop.

"How many did we get?" I could feel more than a handful.

"Oh, I'm not counting, perhaps more than a dozen."

"Are we eating them all for breakfast?" I asked.

"I'll give them to the cook. If we don't have enough, she'll probably make them into omelets."

Isabel led me outside where the early rays of the sunrise, not visible to us yet, illuminated the horizon with pink, orange, and magenta. I could already discern the green leaves from the lower branches of the tall trees.

"I'm getting hungry," I said.

Isabel and I walked up the bamboo steps into the kitchen. I saw our cook, *Aling* Nilda, preparing breakfast by candlelight. I smelled *longanizas*, red native pork sausages, as they made sputtering sounds on the *kawale*, Filipino wok.

"You're up early," *Aling* Nilda said in surprise.

"*Aling* Nilda, I got eggs from under the chickens. It was so much fun. What else are we eating for breakfast? I'm hungry."

"Well, well, well. The country air has certainly given you an appetite, young lady. You never woke up this early for breakfast before. Let's see. For you, I'll make fried eggs, *longanizas*, fried rice, and hot chocolate. How's that?" *Aling* Nilda smiled.

"Thank you very much!" I said, giving her a hug.

"Give me a few minutes to prepare them. The chocolate has already boiled, and *Mang* Antonio has gone to the next farm to buy some *carabao* milk. Sit down. I'll let you whip the chocolate with this beater."

It was a special treat to whip the hot chocolate with a wooden beater to make it fluffy and frothy. What was even more special was to drink the hot chocolate that left a frothy, chocolaty mustache on my upper lip.

"Isabel, will you please get me some water from the well?" *Aling* Nilda asked as she handed a pail to Isabel.

I jumped from my bench. "Can I go with you, Isabel? I'll help you beat the chocolate when I get back, *Aling* Nilda."

"Sure. Come along. You can help with the pumping." Isabel guided me down the bamboo steps. This time, we went to a clearing where an iron pump protruded from a large stone well. She placed my hand on the cold lever and then put hers on top of mine and began pumping it up and down. The lever was heavy, and without her help, I could not have lifted it at all. We pumped it several times before I saw a single drop. Then an icy cold flow of water came out of the spigot.

"Why do we have to get water from the well? Don't we have faucets here like in Manila?" I asked.

"There's no water inside houses in the rural areas. This is just like my home in Ilocos Norte. We have no electricity or water. I have to help my mother get water from the town well."

"Couldn't your mother do it herself?"

"No, she's not strong. She's as frail as your *Inay*. Very thin. My brother and I did the carrying for her. Feel my muscles."

I touched her upper arm. "You are strong, Isabel."

"Let's go up. We have enough water for the kitchen."

"I like you, Isabel. Please don't leave me."

"I won't, unless, of course, my parents ask me to come home. One never knows with this war."

Isabel had been taking care of me since I came to live with my aunt. Looking back on my life, she was the mother I never had, more than my Tia Emilia, who rarely touched me except to discipline me. Isabel fed me, dressed me, bathed me, sang, read and put me to sleep, played with me, scolded me when I misbehaved, and hugged me when I was good. She carried me on her hips, peeled my shrimps and cracked my crabs, separated the bones from my fish meat, and would have spoon fed me had I asked her. In fact, she used to until my brothers teased me about acting like a baby.

I followed Isabel while she did her other chores around the house. Unlike the other maids, she could read, having completed high school. She sometimes read aloud to me the magazines she was reading. Isabel wore her long dark hair in one braid. "To make it appear thick," she would say. She was in her late twenties, unmarried, very affectionate, tall and muscular and very dark. Isabel attributed her dark complexion to the fact that she worked outdoors a lot as a child.

The cool country air and good food made everyone bubbly and talkative during breakfast. Since I had already eaten, I just sat next to my father and listened as my father and siblings talked. It suddenly occurred to me that my father looked more like a grand-father than a father. He was 51 years old. He was clean-shaven, and he had nice white teeth, his own, unusual for many Filipinos his age. His face, neck, and arms were bronzed and wrinkled by the sun. I touched my father's thin gray and black hair, parted on the left, and put my arm around his shoulder. He gave me a smile and patted me on the head. Despite the fear all around us, I remember this tender moment with gladness.

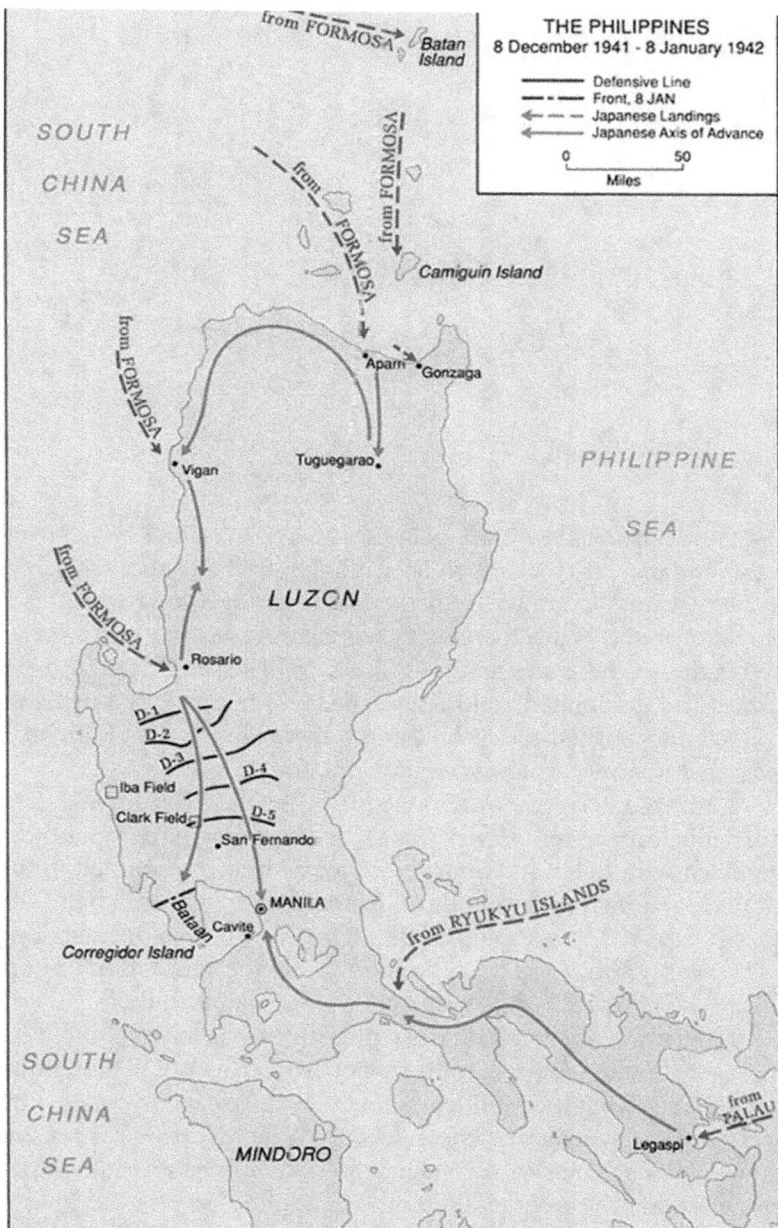

THE PHILIPPINES
8 December 1941 - 8 January 1942

Defensive Line
Front, 8 JAN
Japanese Landings
Japanese Axis of Advance

0   50
Miles

The Japanese Invasion of the Philippines

47

CHAPTER 7

A Few Weeks in Bagbag

I STILL REMEMBER THE TIME IN BAGBAG WITH FONDNESS. There was an abundance of chickens to be slaughtered, fruits and vegetables to be picked. We ate well, for the last time for a long while, as it would turn out. While the men talked, played checkers, and worried about the war, the women, with the help of servants, took care of babies and disciplined children, washed and hung clothes by hand, cooked and washed the dishes, and talked. For us city children, it was a time of new experiences and great fun.

I enjoyed taking showers outside, a new activity for me. The hurriedly improvised shower was made from a large tin tomato can punched with holes and attached to a tree branch. I bathed in my clothes, soaping my thin body and shoulder-length black hair with harsh soap used for washing clothes. The water was cold, but as long as I took my shower in the afternoon under the sun, I didn't mind. But no Ivory or Palmolive soap bars were available to us.

I had always been afraid of heights, but I learned to climb trees in Bagbag. Despite my caution, I fell once from a branch that didn't support my weight. I ended up with bruises on my shin and scratches on my arms and knees. Jeers and laughter from my cousins prevented me from crying. The mango tree, with its spreading thick branches, was the best for climbing. Vic, feeling sorry for me, invited me to join him and Paking on a higher branch that served as their tree house. With Vic's help, I was able to climb to the highest branch

I could reach. What a wonderful feeling to be on top of the world! I could see beyond the treetops, above the roofs of distant huts. I needed help, though, to climb down because I was afraid to fall.

Most of the fruit trees, in addition to the mango, my favorite, were already in bloom but had not borne fruit yet. I was sorry to have missed the mango season in Bagbag, especially after seeing hundreds of blooming mango trees. The tall tree looked pale green from afar, almost white, when it was in full bloom. All I could see were the many small flowers. They exuded a special fragrance and camouflaged the leaves.

I did get to eat lots of guavas, learning how to pick them ripe (they turned from green to yellow and felt squishy) and how to make them fall onto the ground (shake a lower branch) if they were beyond my reach.

Every morning, Isabel gave me corn kernels to throw to the waiting chickens. I even got to help catch them so that we could eat them for lunch. I felt awful and did not look when *Aling* Nilda twisted the chicken's neck and slit it with a sharp knife. I covered my ears so as not to hear the horrible cackling noise of the doomed chicken. But I was fascinated with her efficiency in catching the dripping blood in a bowl with raw rice and then boiling it with salt and spices. The cooked dark blood speckled with white rice was cut up and added to the chicken dish being cooked. It was so delicious. We ate this tasty chicken dish often during the early part of the war, before chicken got scarce.

I even loved eating chicken gizzards. One day, in order to tease me and perhaps discourage me from asking for chicken gizzards so often, *Aling* Nilda showed me how she got the gizzards and what was inside them (chicken waste). My appetite was dampened a bit, but I still eat gizzards, as long as I don't think about where they come from. Also, I make sure I wash them thoroughly even though the butcher has already cleaned them.

I spent the days in Bagbag playing with my older siblings and cousins. Since there were so many of us children, life was never boring. I never lacked for a playmate, but sometimes, because I was the youngest, my siblings excluded me from their games. We played mainly outdoor games like hide and seek among the trees, *piko*, hopscotch, and *patintero*, a common street game.

There was also lots of tree climbing and various expeditions to the interior of the farm. We explored the many hectares of forested and farmed land. Barbed wire fenced the property. We were warned not to climb the fence nor stray outside its boundaries. Branches scratched us as we trampled paths cushioned by last year's leaves and edged with tall wild grasses and weeds that tickled our legs. I learned to identify different fruit trees (mango, *santol*, *siniguelas*) and flowering bushes (*gumamelas*, jasmine, poinsettia, bougainvillea). I listened to various song birds who watched us play, heard the cicadas and crickets, chased multicolored butterflies and moths, captured dragonflies and frogs drinking from a pond and beetles nesting under dead logs. I imitated my brothers who placed the dragonflies in jars and put them indoors at night.

Vic and Paking, showing the entrepreneurial spirit that later helped them in their future business ventures, charged others five centavos to view large beetles engaged in combat inside matchboxes. I never did discover how they made them fight, but the beetles as large as an adult's thumb, with their luminescent black-green hard shells and long spiny antennas, appeared beautiful and invincible locked in combat.

Not all insects were beautiful or interesting. Mosquitoes bit me at night and disturbed my sleep, despite the netting. Mosquitoes entered through the tiniest tear and found any gap between *tatami* and net. Ants, especially the small red ones, swarmed over our legs and bit us during the day when we stumbled onto their nests. They left large welts on my body. My brothers did not complain, but Nena and I cried at the stinging pain, especially when they entered body cavities.

It was easy to urge us to go to bed. When it got dark, we collapsed onto our *tatami* mats, not bothering to bathe or change into night clothes, still wearing our dusty play wear, to sleep deeply until dawn, when the roosters crowed to awaken the whole world.

Although we were out of immediate danger in Bagbag, we did not leave the war entirely behind. One morning, Vic's voice rose above everyone else's. "Papá, the Japanese have landed! I saw a Japanese soldier across the street, on that chicken farm."

Eddy, age 17, who was the acting oldest brother since Hiram joined the Army, answered, "That was our neighbor across the

50

street, Toyo Kusagawa, who is not only a farmer but also a colonel in the Japanese Army."

"Who told you?" asked Paking.

"*Mang* Antonio told me." We all looked at Eddy. He was usually very soft-spoken. He never got angry and was never impatient with us younger children.

"Wow, he must be a spy," Vic said.

"What's a spy?" I asked.

"It's someone who reports everything that he sees and hears to someone in authority," explained Paking.

"Does that mean all the Japanese gardeners in Manila are spies too?" Vic asked.

"Most likely," my father answered.

"Then we can no longer talk if there's a spy near us," I said.

"We should be very careful with what we say and to whom we say it, especially now that we are at war with the Japanese. Even some Filipinos may become enemies," my father said. We all looked at my father and tried to comprehend the seriousness of what he had just said. He looked sad.

One city convenience I missed was the toilet. Since there was no running water in Bagbag, there was no toilet as I knew it in Manila. Instead, there was an outhouse. I insisted that Isabel accompany me whenever I had to use it.

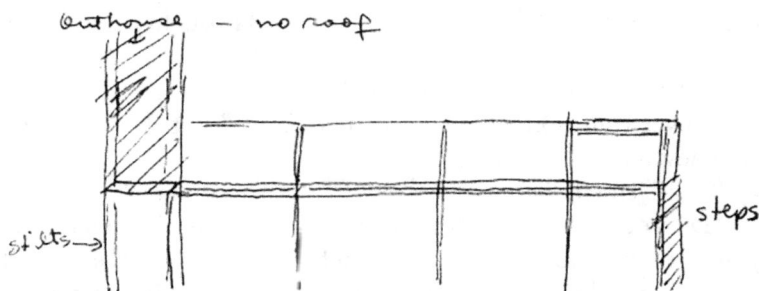

Back home in Manila, we had a regular bathroom with a tiled shower and a ceramic toilet. *Tío* Exequiel's house was next door, and he owned a white ceramic bidet that sprayed water upwards which I loved to use whenever needed. Oh, how I missed that in Bagbag.

The outhouse was set back deep in the woods, quite a distance from the two houses. It was a box-like structure made of thatch and bamboo, standing on stilts, with a door for privacy but no roof. One reached it by going beyond the clearing, climbing up a few steps, and walking on a few bamboo poles tied together to serve as a bridge and approach to the structure. Inside was an upside down wooden box with a hole cut out, to sit on. Cut-up squares of newspapers that served as toilet paper were hard and scratchy.

I was afraid to go there alone and would ask Isabel, "Will you go with me? I have to use the bathroom."

"Oh, Katinka, you're not scared, are you, of going there alone?"

"I am too. It's too far, and I'm afraid of falling down into the hole."

"That hole is too small for you to fall into. But I'll go with you."

Isabel cautioned me, "Watch your step!" as I walked gingerly along the bamboo bridge to reach the outhouse.

"Isabel," I cried as I tried to untie the cotton string that held my underpants (we did not have elastic then). "It's all knotted. I can't untie the knot."

"Oh, Katinka, what will you do without me? Here, let me help you. How come Nena never has a problem untying her pants?"

"She's older," I said, feeling a little bit hurt at the comparison.

"Well, next time, practice how to tie a knot that you can easily untie. I'll show you how." She patiently and adeptly untied the troublesome knot. "I'll wait outside for you. I brought a magazine to read."

"It smells in here!" I complained.

"Cover your nose with your handkerchief." Isabel was very wise and knew a lot of tricks.

"It still smells."

"Do you know how your cousins overcome the smell? They splash cologne on their handkerchiefs so that when they use the handkerchief they cannot smell the stench. Next time, try asking your *Ate* Nene for some of her cologne."

Aside from these inconveniences, there was another reason I was afraid to go to the outhouse. The view from the top provided proper ventilation and a refreshing change of scenery. Many of my cousins would smoke a cigarette secretly while in the outhouse. At times, the view brought fear as well. We could see and hear the Japanese planes flying overhead. Sometimes everyone had to run and hide under the house. The person in the outhouse was often the first person to alert the entire household.

One day while we were there, I heard them myself and called out, "Isabel!"

"What's wrong, Katinka?"

"I hear airplanes," I said.

"I don't see any."

"I hear them, lots of them. Why don't you look up, above the trees? Do you see them now?" The drone of the airplanes got louder. I was frightened they would drop bombs on us in Bagbag.

"Yes, I think I do! Wow, there are lots of them! Maybe more than twenty."

"Where do you think they are going?" I asked.

"They must be on their way to Manila. I'm glad we are not in the city. Why don't you hurry up."

"Do you think they can see us down here?"

"No, I don't think so. They are up high, quite high." Her normally low voice sounded shrill.

I was terrified. I knew they were on a bombing mission to Manila. Even now, whenever I hear a group of airplanes flying overhead, my heart always beats faster as I remember those days and my fear of bombs.

Other than the overhead flights of Japanese airplanes, the war seemed far away. The adults tried to keep abreast of the war news via our radio, but the poor reception prevented them from hearing the most important news.

One day, the farmer next door, *Mang* Pedro, came to the house. He was tall, skinny, and always barefoot. He owned the small parcel of land adjacent to our farm. *Mang* Pedro planted rice and owned a few *carabaos*. He was our source of milk and news. His wife helped *Aling* Nilda in the kitchen sometimes. They had grown-up children who still lived with them.

"Have you heard the news, Mr. Floro?" *Mang* Pedro asked. "They have declared Manila an open city."

"What's an open city?" I asked.

"That means Manila is surrendering and won't retaliate against the airplanes. Consequently, Manila won't be bombed again," explained Paking.

"Does that mean we can go home now?" Nena asked.

"We'll see. Where did you hear this, *Mang* Pedro?" my father asked.

"My son-in-law just arrived from Manila. He said it was all over the city. Are you folks returning to Manila then?"

"Most likely," my father answered. "We'll probably stay around for a few more days, just to make sure it's safe to drive back. Thank you for the news. You have been very kind, supplying us with *carabao* milk. I do appreciate it. Please enjoy some of our fruits when they come out. I have instructed *Mang* Antonio to give you some."

My father shook *Mang* Pedro's hands.

"You are most welcome and thank you. God be with you!" *Mang* Pedro clasped my father's hands and, after releasing them, made a sign of the cross. He left soon after. I don't think he knew that my father was not a religious man.

The day came when my father, as head of the clan, announced that we were returning to our homes in Manila. The news that we would be going home brought cheers to everyone. But I was sad to leave my playground. I had learned to love life in Bagbag.

We returned to Manila to find bombed-out and burnt homes and soldiers everywhere. There were still sporadic bombings. My father had assumed the bombing of Manila would stop, but the Japanese did not honor the Open City declaration. We became apprehensive and nervous as we approached Dimasalang Street. Some empty houses were either burnt to the ground or looted and ransacked. But we were relieved to find our house locked, untouched, and undamaged.

CHAPTER 8

Life in Japanese-Occupied Manila

By THE TIME WE RETURNED FROM BAGBAG, the Japanese Imperial Army had marched into Manila, and news of their atrocities filtered down to us. Details of molestations of women, shooting of civilians, beheadings, and bayonet stabbings of people who wouldn't cooperate with the Japanese passed from neighbor to neighbor.

To control the population and pacify the city, the Japanese Army established neighborhood outposts and sentries. There were two Japanese soldiers at every important intersection, armed with bayonet-tipped rifles, standing guard. Every civilian passing by these soldiers had to stop and bow from the waist down. A Filipino who forgot to bow received a stinging slap on the face. I trembled at the sight of a Japanese soldier. I was afraid of being bayoneted.

I heard the adults talk about "rape," a word unknown to me, and overheard discussions on how to prevent it. At that time, old Filipino women wore a distinctive native dress in two pieces, the long skirt draped by an overskirt and a white thin blouse made of native fibers.

My father and *Tía* Emilia decided that the young women in the family, Nene, Grading, Nenita, as well as the young female servants, would disguise themselves as old women. They had to make themselves look unattractive and old in order to escape the soldiers' attention. It was not possible for them to hide and stay indoors throughout the duration of the war. No one knew how long the war would last. Some thought a few months, at most a year. The Filipinos, including my father, had such great faith in the Americans, especially General Douglas MacArthur. They imagined him recapturing the Philippines in a matter of months, not years.

In order to look old, the young women dyed their hair gray by rubbing wood ashes in it. They wore my aunt's clothing and copied the way she walked: shoulders stooped, head bent, with halting steps. The disguise was put to a test soon afterwards when a platoon of Japanese soldiers stopped in front of our house.

My heart skipped a beat and sweat covered my palms when I saw from an upstairs window the soldiers, dressed in rumpled khaki-colored uniforms drenched in sweat, wearing helmets camouflaged with netting and cut-up twigs and leaves, holding bayonet-tipped rifles, and standing at attention. I thought they were there to arrest my father and my cousin. The officers, who had cleaner uniforms, wore pistols and long swords at their waist, and barked orders in a strange tongue. The words sounded like "kura-kura" to me.

Using hand signals, since no one spoke Japanese in our house, the soldiers asked for water to drink. The soldiers saw only old women working in the kitchen (my young cousins) and took their drink. What a relief to find out they were only thirsty. And yes, they also wanted cooking utensils. They did not want the carbon-charred clay cooking pots used in wood ovens, so our cook willingly gave them the clean-looking *arinolas*, slightly-used white enamel chamber pots.

From an upstairs window, a small voice sang, "God Bless America," recently learned in kindergarten. But before the soldiers could comprehend what was going on, an adult's hand pulled my five-year-old cousin Popoy away from the window and gave him a spanking. The soldiers, not understanding the lyrics in English, looked up, laughed, and then left. Everyone breathed a sigh of relief after the soldiers left. It was a narrow escape. The war would go on for three more years, and there would be more anxious moments for us.

As the war progressed, we started noticing empty window displays and the proliferation of vacant stores due to the scarcity of goods and rampant inflation. *Kokang*, bartering, became the mode of business. Many men lost their jobs. People did not have enough money to buy goods. Even fabric to make clothes became scarce. Housewives started looking at their own treasures and bric-a-brac to barter for food and other necessities. We children imitated the adults. I remember once I bartered a small wooden box that I had treasured as a keepsake for some old comic books to read.

One gets to know a country's economic state from the number and type of people begging on its streets. At first, the Japanese authorities arrested the beggars. Later, as the economy went downhill and because of their sheer numbers, the Japanese tolerated the beggars and left them alone.

Beggars proliferated on the streets. Whereas before the war they only appeared at church steps, now they carried babies on their laps, sang at street corners, and perched across entrances to stores. They even came to the residences to ring bells and beg for food. Even though I was only a child, I was often accosted by beggars of all ages, asking me for food and money. Their bedraggled appearance got worse as time passed. Now those begging on the streets had sores on their hands and faces, part of their flesh eaten by disease, their clothes in tatters, and their voices weak from hunger. I felt sad at seeing those poor souls but was repelled at their sight and foul smell. My father often gave me a few pesos to give to them, but I don't know how much it helped.

Once food became scarce for everyone, not everyone resorted to begging to survive. At the beginning of the war, my father had a small warehouse built between my aunt's house and the courtyard. He used it to store the stockpile of large rolls of white paper needed for his blueprint business. Many burglars mistakenly thought food was stored there. Almost every night, we would find the warehouse broken into and the doors ajar. Nothing would be stolen because it was not humanly possible to carry out those huge rolls of paper.

My father, fearing some disappointed burglars might set fire to the warehouse, installed an alarm system that turned on in his bedroom every time the door to the warehouse was forcibly opened. The first time the alarm tripped, it woke all of us in the house. Fear and confusion filled us. Because of the danger in confronting the burglars, it was decided that only the men, my father and two cousins, would go to the warehouse. They armed themselves with flashlights and large pieces of wood. The burglars, who were unarmed, thank God, were easily caught because the element of surprise was on our side.

I don't remember how I happened to follow my father into the warehouse one night when the alarm was tripped. Their flashlights revealed a frightened old man, surprised by the sudden arrival of my father and cousins, crouched behind a large roll of paper. His dark hair was streaked with gray. He had cracked bare feet and wore a pair of short pants. His shiny brown back was visible beneath a torn shirt.

"Put your hands up!" my father ordered. "What are you doing here?"

"Please, sir. My children have not eaten for two days."

"There is no food here."

"I just found that out, sir. I thought, being a warehouse, it would be full of food."

"You live around here, don't you? I seem to have seen you around."

"I live on Asturias Street, sir. Please don't report me to the police. You know what they'll do to me. My family depends on me."

"I'm glad to see you carry no weapon."

"I meant no harm, sir. We are just hungry."

My father said, "Very well, we will let you go. There's no need to report you to the police, as long as you refrain from burglarizing my warehouse again. On one condition: you must pass the word around that there is no food in this warehouse. There's nothing worth stealing here; there's only paper."

"Sure, patron, I'll pass the word around. Thank you very much for your kindness. May God bless you."

With these parting words, the old man ran out of the warehouse. He did not realize that my father was just as scared as he was that night. I breathed a sigh of relief and went back to the house, to spend much of the night too agitated to sleep further.

The old man kept his word. There were no more midnight visitors, and the burglar alarm did not wake us up again.

The war affected every aspect of our lives, and our childhoods lacked many activities and things most people would consider normal. There were no toys to play with, no parks to visit, no playgrounds for romping, no swimming pools or fishing, no radios to listen to. And yet, we did not lack games to play and playmates to play with. We had cousins, neighbors, and servants for playmates. Everything around us served as toys. We were happy despite the blackness of the situation.

The whole neighborhood became our playground. The unlaid sewer pipes were our jungle gym. On the sidewalks, we played hopscotch, tag, blind man's bluff, and *patinero*, which is a game played by two teams. Each side guards a horizontal line and tries to prevent opposing players from crossing it. The team that is able to cross the line wins. We had no tricycles nor bicycles to pedal, no dolls to play house with, but we used our legs to run and twigs and stones for invented games.

A blackboard cast aside from an abandoned school became our most cherished possession. Our father taught us arithmetic on that blackboard. My favorite was a summation of long rows of numbers. We had contests, aiming for accuracy and speed. Many an unsuspecting cousin came to visit, was challenged to a contest adding rows of numbers, only to be humiliated by the youngest, me. All in all, we children remained resilient despite the hardships we were facing.

CHAPTER 9

The House on Arlegui Street

WHEN MY FATHER PURCHASED THE HOUSE ON ARLEGUI STREET, he did not intend for it to be our family home. He bought it to house his import/export business, his school supply business and the Manila Blue Printing Co. But the war brought a halt to these businesses. There were no goods to import or export. Retail sales of office and school supplies also dried up. No one was building anything. People did not have any money.

When my father heard complaints from his older children regarding conditions at my *Tía* Emilia's house, it convinced him to establish a home for his family sooner than he had planned. Paking and Vic complained of not getting enough food. As growing boys, they were always hungry. The small portions, the lack of second servings, and the favored treatment of my aunt's children at mealtimes reached my father. He found out that my aunt spent most of the money he gave her on her family instead of on us.

Nena and I did not know any of this at the time. We were sad to leave my aunt's house. I really loved her. I was almost seven and still badly in need of a mother's attention. I think our departure left bitter feelings between my father and his sister. What I find strange now is I have no memory of our departure and separation from *Inay*. No matter how hard I try to remember, I can't recall how and when we left. All I remember was the sadness and empty feelings. Fortunately, the sadness turned out to be temporary. There were just too many good things in the huge and wonderful house on Arlegui Street. Also, for the first time, we had enough to eat.

The Arlegui house, built during the Spanish regime, occupied almost a whole block near downtown Manila. A former library for a pharmaceutical firm, it stood at the corner of Arlegui and Gunao streets in the Quiapo district. The second-story floors, made of one-foot wide wood planks, yielded coins, much to our delight, other metallic paraphernalia, and a great amount of dust balls.

Map of present day Manila showing the
locations of the various houses and schools

We learned to love every nook and cranny of the house and pretended we had found pirates' treasure hidden under the flooring. It became my favorite house, and some of the happiest years of my childhood were spent there, despite the war going on all around us. It was so big that we only occupied a small portion of the space. The rest of the house became our playground, a mysterious and wonderful place to explore and play games. Staying indoors during the day no longer bothered us as it had in my aunt's house, crowded with people and hemmed in by rules and restrictions.

The two-story wooden structure with a painted corrugated zinc roof had two sections, each one surrounding an atrium that let in the rain as well as the sun. The back of the building opened out to the *Estero Cegado*, a canal that served as a tributary of the *Pasig* River, the main river that cut Manila into north and south, and unfortunately, provided a source of mosquitoes and sewage smell.

We occupied only the upper story of the northern section of the house. The rest was empty except for the couple who acted as the building's caretakers and their two adopted daughters who lived downstairs by the main entrance on Gunao Street. The oldest daughter, Lita, was about Nena's age. My sister and I were thrilled to have found a playmate living under the same roof.

The house dwarfed us all. A service elevator, hand pulled by two thick rattan ropes, went as far as the second floor. We occasionally got a ride on it whenever the caretaker operated it to transport objects and cargo to be stored in the back rooms of the unoccupied second floor.

A gong, struck by one of the maids, called us to dinner. Food got cold being carried from the back kitchen to the dining room. The living room was the size of a small house. The bedrooms were regular-size except for the huge master bedroom where my father slept. His sparse furniture, consisting only of a double, four-poster bed, an armoire, and a few chairs, made the large bedroom appear even larger.

I loved running to my father's bed on the pretext that mosquitoes had gotten inside my net. "Papá, there is a mosquito inside my bed. It's keeping me awake," I would say and jump onto the bed beside him.

Nena, with whom I shared a bedroom, would also be awakened and would run to join us. "A mosquito bit me too. I can't sleep. Can I also stay with you, Papá?"

Soon, all four of us younger children would crowd into bed with my father. He was very patient with us whenever we disturbed his sleep to complain about mosquitoes.

We played hide and seek in the empty part of the house. The wide wooden columns supporting the beams were so thick a child could hide behind them and not be seen. We sometimes disturbed the bats that nested on the exposed beams and heard their flapping wings as they flew to another part of the house. Sometimes a bat would lose its hold on the beam and fall on the floor. We were warned not to touch or play with the bats, so we avoided them at all cost. I feared them because they reminded me of vampires.

When dusk came and the side street of Gunao became deserted, we played outside on the narrow street. Large cement storm drainpipes as tall as my shoulders stood at the edge of the street, ready to be installed. We used these cement pipes as a base to jump from and reach the iron bars of the windows of the bakery across the street. We dangled with one arm on the iron bars and jumped from bar to bar, laughing and shouting.

One day, *Tía* Emilia was visiting and saw us jumping and hanging from the bars. "What are you children doing? You look like monkeys." She and my father had just come out of the house.

Turning to my father, she said, "Bino, the children shouldn't be climbing and jumping. Look how dirty they are! And it's past five o'clock. They'll certainly catch cold."

"*Ate* Milia—" as he called his elder sister "—you worry too much. The children have been very healthy. The outdoors is good for them. Don't you like their color? They have not been sick since we moved here to Arlegui."

Inay did not say a word. She glanced down and turned away.

"Kiss your aunt and say goodbye, children," my father said, lifting me from the window bar.

We all ran to *Inay*, kissed her cold cheeks, and hugged her thin body.

"Goodbye, *Inay*. We love you. Please come see us again soon," we shouted in unison.

The living room overlooked the busy street of Arlegui. I enjoyed looking out of the window, watching all the people walk by, and hearing the noise of the crowds laughing, talking, and shouting. *Calesas*, pulled by overburdened horses with thin bellies, ferried passengers downtown. It seemed to me that everybody's destination was Quiapo. The crowd did not thin out until quite late at night. Sometimes, I would be awakened from my sleep at around midnight by people shouting and fighting on the street or just laughing and having a good time on their way home. After many months on Arlegui Street, I grew to enjoy the noise of the pedestrians and traffic.

Below our windows, people's heads proved tempting targets for my brothers Vic and Paking. They sprinkled water on them, making people believe it was raining. They laughed at people's different reactions to getting wet. No amount of pleading or threats from Nena and me stopped them. They managed to avoid discovery and continued their pranks until, one day, one of their targets looked up and saw my two brothers in the act of pouring water on pedestrians. The man screamed at them and threatened to report them to the Japanese authorities. The mere mention of the Japanese terrified my brothers. The threat of a police arrest put a stop to their antics. They never played tricks on pedestrians again.

One day, my father's caretaker from Laguna brought a truck full of mangoes to our house and before my father could give most of them away, the mangoes filled one of the empty rooms in our house on Arlegui Street. The room was knee-deep in mangoes, piled neatly on top of each other, in various state of ripeness. The unripe green ones could be eaten, but they were very tart and had to be salted. One ate green mangoes occasionally, to be dipped in salt or vinegar. It was better to wait for them to ripen, when they exuded this sweet fragrance only a mango could give, and turned yellow with a little sprinkling of black dots. After the rationing of mangoes in my *Inay's* house, this was heaven.

For several days, my brothers, sisters, and I would sneak into the "mango" room, carefully choosing the large, ripe ones, then eating them whole by peeling the skin first, savoring and biting into the sweet fleshy parts, and discarding the fibrous pits. They were so sweet.

I could eat three or four in one sitting and then return for more later in the day. I do not remember how many mangoes I ate that week, but it was a lot, enough to give me a stomachache and diarrhea that lasted for another week.

The *lanzones* season came in December. They are yellow clustered fruits the size of large grapes. The opaque sectioned pulp, studded with bitter seeds, was juicy and sweet. My father's orchard in Laguna, famous for the best variety of *lanzones*, yielded dozens of bushels of the yellow fruit for us to enjoy. Since they came before the Christmas season, he gave most of them away as gifts to relatives and friends. My father was very concerned with the damage done by bats to his *lanzones*. He often wished someone would invent a device that would either lure the bats away or make them sterile. He felt this would have been an invention worth millions to farmers.

I associate the house on Arlegui Street with another major loss from my childhood. I was very close to my nursemaid Isabel. Over the years, I often begged her not to leave me. She always assured me she would stay with me as long as she was needed but that if her parents called her home, she had to obey them and go. I knew how much she loved her mother, who was sickly, because she often told me stories about her and showed me her picture. I envied her relationship with her mother. I hoped and prayed they wouldn't call her home.

But unfortunately, the day did come when they sent word that she was needed at home. How I cried, for days, when I found out she was leaving us. Her mother was very ill and she had to go. She couldn't promise that she would be back. The war made it impossible for her to make future plans.

I remember clearly the day of her departure. A typhoon was brewing somewhere in the Pacific, and rain was pelting us day and night. I worried that Isabel would not reach her home because of the strong winds and rain. But she reassured us the road would be passable and the bus she was to take would arrive safely in her hometown.

The tradition in our house was that every maid's belongings had to be inspected by the woman of the house before the maid was allowed to leave. I guess this was to prevent the departing maid from stealing valuables from us. I learned later on that many Filipino families followed this tradition. Since we didn't have a mother to do this, it fell on the oldest daughter, Fe. Years later after Fe left home, Nena and I did the "honors" of inspecting a maid's belongings.

Isabel had packed her meager belongings into a worn-out woven *buri* satchel that she must have brought into our house when she first arrived. Its edges, frayed and raveling, had to be tied with a string to hold its contents together. She arranged about six faded cotton dresses inside the satchel, most of which I recognized as having been gifts from *Inay*. A pair of brown sandals, a hand-me-down from Fe, stood forlorn on the table. Because of the bad weather, Isabel would not wear her sandals on her trip home; she would use her wooden *bakya*. She used the shoes only for going to Mass on Sundays. She told me she was saving them for her homecoming when her family most likely would give a feast in her honor. She promised to write to me about it.

I stood by the table, my head barely able to clear the top. I watched and cried as Isabel lifted each dress to show there was nothing of ours hidden in between the clothes. A face powder compact and a few barrettes to hold her braid rattled in a little box Grading had discarded years ago. I saw a familiar face on a faded sepia picture, that of her mother. Isabel was a young version of her mother. She had often showed me this picture whenever we talked about her family.

I continued to sob as the short ritual took place. I cried at losing Isabel. I was too young to recognize the indignity she had to endure, considering how long she had been with us. But Isabel knew this had to be done for all departing servants. She didn't say anything. Nena gave her a small pin with a fake pearl, a favorite of hers, as a parting gift. My father gave Isabel an extra month's salary, and I gave Isabel a small photograph of the two of us so that she wouldn't forget how I looked.

I cried louder as Isabel hugged me to say goodbye. She hugged me tightly, tears streaming down her face, and promised to look us up after the war. Both my father and Isabel had to reassure me that Isabel would return for a visit after a while. I ran to the window overlooking Arlegui Street to shout and wave goodbye. My father had given her a red umbrella to protect her from the rain. From the window, I watched her red umbrella twirling in the rain as it disappeared into a sea of mist and black umbrellas. Rain was coming through the window, wetting my face, already soaked with tears. But I didn't leave the window for a long time after the red umbrella disappeared from sight. I never had a nursemaid again.

We never heard from nor saw Isabel again. I continued to hope and wait to hear from her, but even inquiries sent to her home went unanswered. My father surmised that she and her family might have died during the liberation of the Philippines.

CHAPTER 10
Hiram's Death March

IN APRIL AND MAY OF 1942, THE BATAAN PENINSULA and Corregidor Island fell to the Japanese. Although it was a loss, for our family, it meant the promise of my oldest brother Hiram's return from war. Hiram was the oldest, my half-brother who was thirteen years older than me. I worshipped him. He protected me from my other siblings whenever there was a fight. Vic and Paking often bossed me around and made fun of me. But Hiram always took my part. I especially looked forward to his arrival home from school because he loved to tell me stories.

I felt that we shared a common bond even though he was the oldest while I was the youngest. He, too, had lost his mother. Not through death but because his mother, my father's young, beautiful first wife, Naomi, abandoned Hiram after he was born. I was told she did not want to have any responsibilities, especially that of being a mother. My father had to hire a wet nurse to breastfeed him.

Hiram was not a very good student. He did not like to study, so he often failed his classes in school. The word in Tagalog for to fail and to fall is the same, *bumagsag*, so that whenever someone would comment that Hiram had failed in school again, I had visions of him falling out of the school building. I wondered why he did not hurt himself.

A year before the outbreak of the war, Hiram fell madly in love with a beautiful seventeen-year-old *Sabbadista* (Seventh Day Adventist) named Nenita, who lived a few blocks from our house by the Dimasalang Bridge. I saw Nenita for the first time one evening when I heard sobs coming from the living room of my aunt's house. Nenita and her parents were seated opposite Hiram and my father. While most girls her age wore their hair in braids, Nenita wore her long brown hair loose, falling down to her waist. Her simple frock emphasized her tiny figure and long legs. From the furtive glances she gave my brother, I saw a smile that lit up a pair of light brown eyes surrounded by the longest lashes I had ever seen.

Nenita's mother was crying. I knew Hiram had been gone for a while, but I did not know where. But I soon found out that he and Nenita had just returned from an elopement. It was then common in the Philippines for a young couple to run away if the parents did not approve of the marriage. After a few days and nights of living together, they returned home so that the parents had no choice but to consent to a wedding.

Since Nenita's mother continued to cry, I heard Hiram say in a loud voice, "If you wish, you can have Nenita back; then we don't have to get married." I saw a smile break out on my father's lips.

Upon hearing these words, the mother cried louder so that in the end, Nenita and Hiram were married. My father, since he was not Catholic, did not object to Nenita and Hiram being married under the Seventh Day Adventist rites. Only my devoutly Catholic aunt Emilia objected to the marriage.

Despite the intense love between Nenita and Hiram, the marriage was not a happy one. From the very beginning of their marriage, they never had any privacy. Hiram depended on my father for financial support, so they lived with him, which was then the custom. The lack of privacy and Hiram's immaturity led to disharmony and constant bickering. Sharing a house with relatives caused more turmoil, leading Hiram to escape his home and enlist in the Philippine Scouts shortly after his son Herman was born. Nenita and Herman continued to live with us after Hiram joined the Army.

We knew Hiram's unit had surrendered to the Japanese at Bataan, and that meant he would be a prisoner of war. My father had explained to us about the Geneva Convention and that it required captured prisoners to be treated humanely. At the time, we felt relief that Hiram would no longer be fighting and risking his life.

The Bataan Death March

When the Japanese invasion of the Philippines reached the Bataan Peninsula, the two sides met at the Battle of Bataan in 1942. The allied forces lost this battle, and the Army of the Empire of Japan forced the survivors on a cruel and arduous march from the Bataan Peninsula to Camp O'Donnell located sixty miles north. A total of sixty to eighty thousand prisoners from the Bataan Peninsula were marched to this camp, which was occupied by the Japanese Army.

The march gained its notoriety and its name due to the treatment of the prisoners, mostly American and Philippine soldiers. Prisoners who were unable to keep up with the gruelling pace were shot on the spot, and those who attempted to escape were shot as well. Sympathetic civilians who attempted to help were at risk to lose their lives, or worse, as a reprimand by the Japanese.

At no point did the Japanese Army abide by the Geneva Convention, the rules that govern warfare between nations. They marched the men hours on end without letting them take any drinks of water under the hot sun, fed them little to nothing, and provided no care to injuries they suffered. They were forced to stand still in one position for long periods of time, being tortured in some cases if they did something as simple as shifting their weight from one leg to the other.

The exact death toll from the march remains unknown, as despite these brutal conditions, some were able to escape. The amount of people simply killed on the march was also not documented. Those who survived and did not escape were interned at Camp O'Donnell.

We found out later that the captured soldiers, about seventy thousand Americans and Filipinos, many sick with malaria and weak from lack of food, were forced to march to a prison camp in Tarlac, sixty miles away. This became known as the Bataan March or the Death March because so many, perhaps as many as ten thousand, mostly Filipinos, died along the way. My family believed, although we never found out for certain, that my brother Hiram was among those who fell in the Death March.

When no official word came to us regarding Hiram's fate, my father made it known that he would pay for any information about my brother. He believed that Hiram was still alive somewhere, perhaps hiding and living among people who escaped into the jungle to fight the Japanese, and would return sometime after the end of the war.

He followed all leads about him, giving money and clothing to anyone who said he had seen him in such and such province. I remember one visitor in particular. We were in the living room of the Arlegui house in Quiapo one Sunday afternoon when the doorbell rang. Nena and I were practicing a duet on the piano, Fe was reading, and my father and brother Eddy were teaching Vic and Paking how to play chess. Rosa, a new maid, brought in an old thin man with a prominent fresh scar that ran diagonally across his left cheek. He wore his Sunday best, clean but tattered clothes, and was holding a native hat in his hands.

He bowed his head before my father and said, "Mr. Floro, I understand you have been looking for your son who was a volunteer with the Scouts. My name is *Kapitan* (Captain) José Lauria."

My father stood up from his chair, greeted the old man with a smile, and shook his hand. "Please sit down, *Kapitan*. May I offer you something to eat or drink?"

"Thank you very much, sir. You are very kind. A glass of water will be fine." He took a seat on the rattan armchair opposite the two couches where we all sat. Nena and I sat beside my father, nervously eyeing the new visitor.

"Rosa, will you please bring the captain a glass of water?" Turning to Vic, "Why don't you get Hiram's picture to show *Kapitan* Lauria? Tell Nenita to come and meet him."

"Nenita went out with the baby and won't be back until after dinner," Fe said.

I saw a flicker of disappointment in my father's eyes, but he did not say anything. He took the picture of Hiram and showed it to the old man.

"Have you seen my son? His name is Hiram Floro; he has no nickname. He's tall and thin, just turned twenty years old. He was born in Manila and speaks only Tagalog. He is dark and has also dark curly hair."

"He eats hard boiled eggs and swallows them whole," I blurted out, causing embarrassed smiles to break out on everyone's faces.

"I don't think *Kapitan* Lauria is interested in hearing that," Fe said.

"Well," Nena added, "he has a cute baby who got very sick with polio and almost died. He's okay now, but his left leg is shriveled."

"Children, I think *Kapitan* Lauria now has a picture of what Hiram looks like," my father said patiently. He turned to the captain and continued, "We were told he was with a Philippine battalion that surrendered to the Japanese in Bataan. I have spoken to the authorities, Filipino as well as Japanese, but they all say his name does not appear in any of their official lists."

"I may have some news for you. I saw your son in Bataan, a few days before we surrendered. He was sent to our unit by his captain to ask for medical supplies. I remember him because he looked so young. I even asked him for his age. That's when he told me his name and where he was from."

"How was he when you saw him?" asked my father, happy and a little excited to finally meet someone who had seen Hiram.

"He seemed well, except very haggard-looking, as we all were at the time." *Kapitan* Lauria looked down at his bony hands, darkened by the sun. "By then we all were suffering from malnutrition. There was no food available, and I remember telling your son to start fishing for food. He laughed at this. I think he thought I was making a joke."

We all laughed too.

"That sounds like Hiram all right." My father smiled. "Did you have any further communication with him or his unit after that?"

"I'm afraid the next two days have become a blur in my memory. I heard their unit was captured first. They put up a great deal of resistance and sustained heavy casualties. My unit, fortunately or unfortunately, depending on one's point of view, was captured with light casualties because we were ordered to surrender immediately."

My father inched forward from his position on the couch. He looked straight into the captain's eyes and asked, "What do you think happened to my son?"

The captain coughed and tried to clear his throat. "If he were still alive when their unit was captured, he could have escaped and joined the guerrillas into the mountains. He'll probably wait out the war there. I understand a lot of our comrades have gone into the jungle to form guerrilla units and fight the Japanese there. Had he been captured alive, he would have marched to Capas, and his name would have appeared on the official list of prisoners. But had he been captured while wounded, he may not have survived the march. It was during the march where most of the wounded died." He lowered his gaze and looked down on the floor.

I gasped, and the old man looked at me with sad eyes.

He continued. "Everything turned to chaos days before we surrendered. There was no food, no replacement for ammunition. Somehow the food and medical supplies promised never got to us in Bataan. We were eating leaves and roots; others were lucky to have caught fish to eat. The fighting was ferocious. We were face to face with the enemy. A lot of my comrades were killed right in front of me."

He took out a clean but wrinkled handkerchief with a big rip in the center and wiped his face. I held on to my father's left hand tightly. It was moist and tense. I no longer could look at the captain's face; instead, I stared at my bare feet, quietly touching the wool Chinese floral rug in the center of the living room. It felt rough but pleasant.

"Do take your time. Would you like a glass of lemonade to clear your throat? Fe, tell Rosa to bring a glass. Perhaps she can bring us all some."

We were all seated around the old man, eyes and ears glued to his face. He put his left hand on his scar as he was talking. I tried not to look at it, but it was such a long one I couldn't help but stare.

The glasses clinking against the lemonade pitcher as Rosa brought in the refreshments broke the stillness in the room. I rushed to get a glass after giving the first glass to the captain. His throat had dried up with his narration, and he hurriedly finished the sour lemonade. He coughed afterward, and I was glad he did not choke.

"Thank you, that feels good. It's just ... telling the story brings it back. But I must get it out of my system."

Tears welled in his eyes. He cleared his throat and continued. "We were given orders to surrender after we heard the news that

General MacArthur had left for Australia. They kept telling us that a ship would come and pick us up, but it never came. We thought at least surrendering to the Japanese would help our sick and wounded, that we would be given food. That turned out to have been a mistake. The Japanese soldiers are trained to fight to the death and never surrender. So, they looked down on those who do. They thought we were ... unworthy."

He paused and looked at his surroundings. The sun had begun to set, and the noise from the street below had died down. He looked beyond the open windows and seemed to be reading the clouds. "Were we ever wrong! The Japanese Army is the most brutal I have ever known. Their soldiers are worse than animals. During the march to Capas, for six days, we did not get food or water. But the worst part was the killing of the wounded. Anyone who could not keep up with the march, who fell behind from illness, wounds, or weakness, was bayoneted by those brutes. Anyone who even asked for water was killed and left by the side of the road." He was almost shouting. He stopped and checked himself.

"I did not mean to shout and get you into trouble, Mr. Floro. You know there are spies everywhere. But what happened to us is embedded in my mind forever; I can't forget it. After I leave here, I'm going north to join some of my men." I saw his face relax briefly. Even his scar seemed to close and disappear.

"Do you think Hiram could have been one of those men killed along the way?" my father asked. I did not want to hear the captain's reply because I was afraid it would be bad news, but I couldn't move.

"I really can't be too sure. Had he been among the wounded, he surely would have been killed by the Japanese during the march. But if he were among the lucky few saved by some of the villagers along the way, then he might be living among them now, recovering from his wounds."

I saw a glimmer of hope in my father's eyes. Even I relaxed a bit upon hearing this bit of news. "How do you know that?" asked my father.

"You see, many people along the way tried to save some of the fallen and wounded. Villagers came out, risked their lives to give food and water to us, especially at night. But the Japanese shot or bayoneted those they caught feeding or helping one of us." I looked up at the captain. His face was twisted. He seemed in a great deal of pain.

"I am sorry for what I have to say now, but it's the truth. I saw some villagers' bodies hanging from trees. I saw others with their heads or legs cut off, lying by the side of the road. I was told that was to teach them a lesson not to help us. Would you believe the Japanese trucks and tanks even ran over bodies who might have been still alive! I cannot forget it. I cannot forget it. It was awful." He covered his face with his brown hands. He began to sob. We all started to cry as well.

I pictured an endless number of trucks and tanks trying to run over live people. I couldn't imagine anything worse than this. I cried uncontrollably.

My father stood and touched his shoulder. "You poor, brave soul. I am so sorry to hear of your terrible ordeal. It's so horrible. And my poor son, to think how he must have suffered." It was all that my father could say. He was also in tears. He looked at us. I was afraid he would send us to our room. I had to hear the old man's story.

The captain said, "I'm truly sorry to be distressing all of you, especially the children."

"Children," my father said, "you may go to your rooms if the *kapitan's* story is upsetting you."

"Papá, we want to know what happened to Hiram. We want to stay," Vic said. We all nodded in unison.

"Very well, then, you may all stay," my father said to us. "Please continue, *Kapitan*. Whatever you tell us will remain within these walls—I want to assure you. I thank you for telling us what must be very painful for you to remember. I know war is cruel, but I did not know how cruel man could be to his fellow men. I will understand if you stop now."

"No, no, Mr. Floro, I want to tell people what happened, but I have to be careful to whom I tell it. I don't want to go back to prison. Before I came here, I asked around, and I have been told by my comrades that you and your family are to be trusted. Even though I knew your son very briefly, I feel that by telling you what happened, it may give you more leads in finding him."

My father smiled. "Thank you very much, *Kapitan*. We are eternally grateful to you. My children and I will honor your request. Children, you will not talk about what you are hearing now to others. We do not want the captain to get into trouble. We want Hiram back, and the captain's story will help us find him."

We all nodded our heads. I wanted Hiram back. I missed him a lot. I missed his stories, his jokes, and his protection.

After a sip of his lemonade, the old man continued his story, how he survived the march and made it to Capas, Tarlac where all the prisoners were held. The brutality of his Japanese captors continued while he was in Capas. The Filipino and American soldiers were tortured and starved. More soldiers died due to illness and starvation during their captivity. Some months later, some of the men were released, and he was one of the lucky ones still alive to be set free. He still suffered from malaria and the lingering effects of malnutrition and torture.

It had gotten dark. I could hear the maids setting the dinner table. My father invited the captain to stay for dinner, and he accepted. He was silent during the meal and no longer talked about his experiences. He kept muttering that he owed everything to God. We found out he was only in his forties; his rumpled, dried skin made him look sixty. My father offered him some clothes and money. He did not want to accept, but my father insisted. His story, though quite painful, gave my father some understanding of what could have happened to my brother.

We prayed that Hiram was alive and had joined the guerrillas in the mountains. Or if he had been captured, he could have been one of the soldiers saved by the villagers. My father hoped against hope that some local people took him in, helped him survive. Some did survive the march as in the case of *Kapitan* Lauria.

After the captain's departure, no one spoke until my father wondered out loud how the Japanese he met in Tokyo on a previous trip before the war could be so disciplined, respectful, and peaceful compared to the cruel and inhuman soldiers. "Could there be two Japans?" he asked aloud.

I was next to him and did not reply. No one knew the answer to his question.

As the war progressed, our hopes for Hiram's return dimmed. When the war ended, Hiram was officially declared missing in action and presumed dead. Life would never be the same again for all of us.

After the war, I relived some of the horrors of the war by seeing movies made about the Japanese occupation of the Philippines. I read authors who interviewed many soldiers and former prisoners of war. They said that, had they known their fate at the hands of the Japanese Army, they would have gladly killed themselves rather than surrender. At the time, the government estimated that twenty-five thousand men died during the march. Later the estimates were dropped to six to ten thousand. I had nightmares for months after hearing and reading all these horrible things and imagining what had happened to my brother, who used to sit me on his lap and make funny faces at me while telling me stories.

CHAPTER 11
School Days

SCHOOL WAS ANOTHER PART OF OUR CHILDHOOD that was greatly affected by the Japanese occupation. Going to school was an adventure. You never knew where your classes would be held. The Japanese made elementary schools their army headquarters. At first, we shared our buildings with them. Later on, they just pushed the schoolchildren out, and other places had to be found for their schooling. I guess they wanted to protect their headquarters from being bombed, knowing that the Americans would not bomb hospitals, churches, or schools.

Even though I was six, I missed being placed in first grade before the war because I failed the entrance test: I couldn't place my right hand across the top of my head to touch my left ear. That was how they determined one's readiness for first grade in those days. It did not seem to matter that I could already read some newspaper articles in Tagalog and do simple addition. I stayed another year in kindergarten, coloring, counting, and relearning the ABC's.

So I did not start first grade until after 1942, the year we moved to the house on Arlegui Street. We were assigned to go to Apolinario Mabini Elementary School on Quezon Boulevard, a very busy street in the Quiapo district. It was a two-story wooden building adjoining another building that housed a police station. The grounds were large but bare. Not a single bush or grass grew anywhere.

Although school was quite a distance from our house, my siblings and I enjoyed our walk to school, but it was not without its dangers. We snaked our way through crowds in the downtown district, loitering at windows of countless shops with different items for sale, pausing to smell dried fish and *bagoong*, fermented fish sauce, at food stalls. We longingly admired unattainable dolls and trucks displayed in windows of toy stores. Asian-faced mannequins dressed in utilitarian clothes from Japan started appearing in store windows. Many signs in Japanese using Chinese characters appeared alongside Tagalog. English disappeared from conversations, reading materials, and advertisements. The sidewalks were lined with illegal vendors selling all kinds of goods in woven rattan baskets, so it was like walking on a tightrope to maneuver in the remaining space.

The entertaining walk to school was marred one day by an unfortunate incident with a peanut vendor. That day, I was distracted as usual, looking all around me as I walked, marveling at the food and toys for sale. I did not notice the lace edge of my skirt's hem had caught one of the rattan baskets filled with peanuts. My skirt dragged the basket and spilled its contents onto the sidewalk. The seller, a tall, burly man, screamed at me and demanded payment for all the peanuts that were spilled. Isabel stood her ground and protected me, laying the blame for the mishap on the vendor's illegal placement on the narrow sidewalk. I was so scared and feared for my life because the man was livid with anger. I thought he would kill me. After that, I asked that we not walk on that particular sidewalk because I was afraid the man would remember me and either beat me up or accost me for payment.

Another day, a truck stopped on the street in front of us to unload some soldiers armed with bayonet-tipped rifles. The soldiers pushed us against the wall and made us stand facing away from the street. I was so terrified my knees became weak. I was certain we would be shot. Everyone was ordered to face the wall. Soon the sound of sirens replaced the barking shouts of the soldiers. I surreptitiously took a sidelong glance to find out what was going on, not fully aware of the consequences of my action. A motorcade passed by, Japanese and Filipino flags flying from the hood of a black limousine. Inside the car sat a Japanese officer, perhaps a general, and a bespectacled Filipino in a white suit.

I learned later that I had seen in person the puppet President of the Philippines, Dr. José P. Laurel. The Japanese believed their Emperor descended from God, so that no mortal being was permitted to lay eyes on him. Our Philippine President was not descended from God, as we all knew, but to command respect for him, the military leaders made sure the Filipinos did not lay eyes on him. We were all forced to look away from the street whenever his motorcade passed by. After the war, Laurel was charged with collaborating with the enemy. He was acquitted and ran successfully for the Philippine Senate. He claimed he was only following orders of his predecessor, President Manuel Quezon, who had escaped to America. Many people were tried as collaborators after the war. Even a well-known society woman, who got rich by being a mistress to a Japanese general, was tried in court. She also was acquitted. She kept her ill-gotten riches.

One day, upon arriving at school after heavy rains caused the *Estero Cegado* to overflow its banks and flood some of the streets in Quiapo, we found our schoolmates milling around the building next to our school. The building was a police outpost, and on what was normally a flag hanging from a flagpole, I saw the first and still largest python I have ever seen dangling from the pole. The snake, almost as tall as the second floor balcony, had been swept by the floodwaters into the orchestra pit of the Times Theater in downtown Quiapo. An usher, who was sweeping the mud off the floor of the theater, saw it slithering along the aisle after the floodwaters had receded and called the police. It took several men to capture and kill it.

Even in death, it caused fear among us children. Its head with bulging eyes dangled from a noose, its fat greenish tail almost touching the ground. Rumors circulated that they had found a dog inside its belly. Tales were told of finding *carabaos*, water buffaloes, inside some pythons. I used to have nightmares about that snake.

In school, the children in the older grades were taught how to read and write in Japanese. Since I was only in first grade, I learned how to write and read Tagalog. But in gym class, we learned to count up to eight in Japanese because that was how far we counted in calisthenics. I've not forgotten it. I can still count up to eight in Japanese.

The Japanese had not yet had time to acquire or write new textbooks for us, so they were forced to use our old American textbooks from years past. However, the books were censored. The Japanese government felt very strongly that the Filipinos should forget the Americans. They tried to teach us that the Americans would never return and that we should learn to live with and love our Asian brothers, the Japanese.

Every page in our textbooks that mentioned America or Americans was covered with a piece of white paper. Sometimes, there would be consecutive pages all covered with white paper. It became very difficult to make sense out of what we were reading. Out of curiosity, I used to peek at the censored pages and, some-times, tore them out in order to see what was forbidden. I soon found out that anything that said the words "American," "U.S.A.," "President Roosevelt," "President Quezon," or anything American or related to the previous Philippine government was either crossed out or covered. I could not understand then why such words were forbidden, but I quickly decided that they must be important and desirable.

At the end of the school year, my siblings and I all topped our respective grades and were awarded prizes at a public ceremony on the school grounds. Fe turned out to be the best student in Japanese. I used to look at Fe's Japanese books and was confused to find it going from back to front, right to left. For my achievement, I received a second grade writing pad. I was looking forward to second grade, but the Japanese Army decided to take over our school building and use it for an army barracks. I was so sad to hear that we could no longer attend school. It appeared then that our school days were over.

Fortunately, my father offered the downstairs of the Arlegui house for use as a school. The school authorities thanked him for his generosity and accepted his offer. Part of the unoccupied downstairs became the neighborhood elementary school and I started second grade there. I loved having school in my own house. What a joy not to worry about being late. I could wake up as late as possible in the morning and still not miss the opening bell. All I had to do was walk down the stairs. During recess, if I got hungry, I simply went upstairs for a snack. Kids envied me. I felt important because my house was our school.

During school days, the place was noisy with the sound of children and teachers. It was a very informal school. Teachers seemed more relaxed even though they encountered disciplinary problems with some students. Everyone was happy that we were still able to continue school despite the Japanese taking over the other building. Since the Arlegui house had no outside yard for playing, we spent our recess playing on granite blocks in the atrium. This happiness lasted almost a whole year.

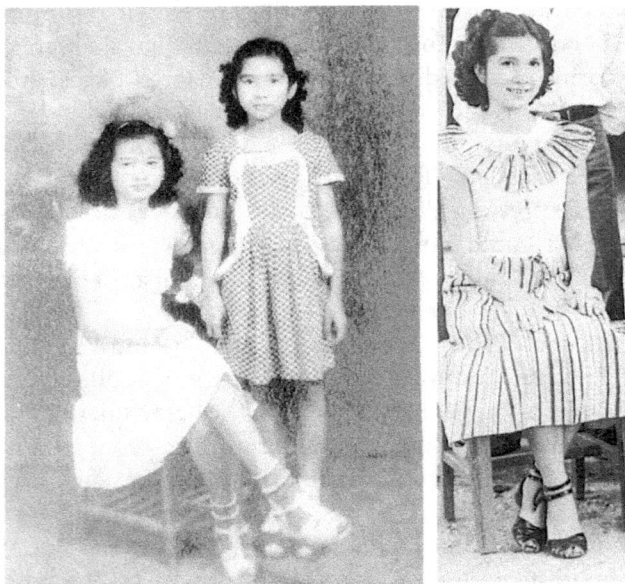

Nena and Katinka in the 1940s (left); Katinka as a teen (right)

My elementary school years were also a time of learning to play the piano and furthering my love of music. When I was five, whenever I saw a piano keyboard, either real or even an image in a magazine, I would bang on it, pretending to be playing. I was obsessed. Any piano sound attracted my attention, and I stopped whatever I was doing in order to listen. I still do. I can still be transfixed by the sound of a piano concerto.

In my *Inay's* house where we lived, even touching the black grand piano in the living room was forbidden to children. How I longed to play it, but *Inay* was very strict. She said that children might leave dirty finger marks on the shiny ebony wood or mar the cream ivory keys. A servant dusted it every morning.

The piano was a present for *Inay's* daughter-in-law, Nene. She never had music lessons, but she could play by ear any tune she heard, on the piano as well as on the guitar. Whenever I heard the music, I would run downstairs to sit by her side as she played and sang. She would even teach me the names of the notes: "do, re, mi…" She always let me sit by her side as she played. She showed me how to listen to a song and find the corresponding sound on the keyboard. I loved hearing her long manicured fingernails making clicking sounds on the keys as she played. As long as I was by her side, I did not fear my *Inay's* wrath as I touched the smooth black and white keys and experimented with the different sounds each key produced.

Then one Christmas—the one before Pearl Harbor—my father gave me my first piano. It was a black wooden toy piano, not more than a foot wide, containing a keyboard of two octaves. I would sit on the floor for hours and play on it. I learned to play on my piano with one finger any song that I could sing. The black keys were only painted on. I can still hear the tinny, high-pitched notes of that toy piano. Later on, people told me I had perfect pitch. But then, all I knew is that I could finally make music on my own, and forget the world around me.

After we moved to Arlegui Street, my father bought us a real "live" piano, a tall upright made of ebony, with two pairs of brass candelabras attached to the front panel, and a three-legged stool on wheels that revolved up and down for seat adjustment. The candelabras, although originally decorative, ended up proving useful. As electricity began to be rationed, the lighted candles enabled us to play the piano in the dark.

The piano occupied a prominent place in our large living room on Arlegui Street. It sat on a pastel Chinese wool area rug, flanked by two rattan couches with floral cushions and a glass-topped coffee table, also made of rattan. The piano became the center of attraction as every visitor who came to the house was urged to perform on it.

Cousin Terry played "Liebestraum" and another cousin played "Moonlight Sonata" on every visit.

Miss Luming came into our lives in 1942. She taught us piano once a week. She gave Paking, Nena, and me each one hour of her time. I was as afraid of her as I had been of *Inay*. She was in her forties, dark complexioned, with very sharp eyes, short, and a little heavy around the hips from sitting too long on piano benches. Her hands were long, and her fingernails were cut short. On several occasions, I had to cut my fingernails before I could begin my lessons. She did not tolerate long fingernails on any piano student of hers.

Although I enjoyed playing, I suffered through the learning and fingering processes. I did not understand why I had to practice the scales, the exercises in the Czerny and Hanon collections, and sing from the Solfeggio. I only wanted to learn how to play Chopin's "valses" or Beethoven's sonatas. Every lesson, Miss Luming scolded me for not practicing my exercises. When playing a piece, Miss Luming would slap my fingers every time I used the wrong finger on a note.

One particular day, I was not prepared for my lessons. I spent some time flipping the pages of the Czerny book, looking for the assigned pieces.

Miss Luming tapped my hands and looked into my eyes. "You have not touched the piano this week, have you, Katinka?"

"No, Miss Luming."

"Katinka, how many times have I told you that you have to practice every day to play well?"

"Miss Luming, I'm sorry. I know what you mean, but sometimes I just can't seem to get started."

"Your problem is you are too lazy to practice. I hope next time you'll be better prepared. Now, let's repeat this week's assignment for next week. And don't forget to practice." She wrote an "R" for repeat on the music piece. Most of my assigned music pieces had red "R"s beside the name of the piece.

"I won't, Miss Luming. Thank you," I said, half-smiling. I was expecting a more severe punishment than the scolding she gave me. I was relieved that Miss Luming did not vent more of her anger on me that day.

Some weeks, I worked hard at my piano assignments, practicing every day. I expected her to notice, but she never said anything when I did well. Then, laziness set in, and I stopped practicing again. Then she would get angry at me, and the entire lesson would be filled with her scolding and slapping my fingers. The angrier she got, the lazier I became.

Miss Luming may not have been an inspiring piano teacher, but she was a very accomplished pianist. I loved listening to her play. She always showed us how to play a piece before she assigned it. I always looked forward to this. Often, I would request her to play several pieces for me before we started my lessons.

Miss Luming discouraged us from playing any other kind of music than our assignments. One day, she heard my brother Paking and me play a duet of "Chopsticks." Miss Luming got very angry. I did not understand. We thought we were making beautiful music. She felt that improvising on the keyboard, which we sometimes did, would ruin our fingering. She despised jazz. Only classical music would do for her. But she did help me develop my perfect pitch and encouraged me to sing out the notes.

Despite the anguish of practice, I did experience my first piano recital under Miss Luming's guidance. However, I almost did not make it to the recital due to an accident shortly beforehand. The accident happened at high noon, on a hot sunny day in April, in downtown Manila, during the Japanese occupation. I was not a casualty of street fighting, even though I had sometimes seen Japanese sentries posted around Manila firing their weapons. I was in a tram accident. My brother Paking, sister Nena, and I were riding an electric tram that circled Manila on our way to our final piano rehearsal for the recital when we missed our stop. Panicked at getting lost, my brother told us to jump from the moving tram. Nena and I jumped after him, but I missed my step and landed flat on my face. Luckily, I did not break any bones, but I scraped my knees very badly and bled profusely. I skinned my elbows and had a few cuts on my chin.

I cried at the sight of blood oozing down my elbows and knees and from the pain inflicted by the hot asphalt. A crowd of curiosity-seekers gathered around us. Finally, an elderly woman in black rescued us. She took me in her arms, consoled me, and with her scented and embroidered white linen handkerchief, wiped off my tears and blood. After making sure that we were not seriously hurt, she commanded someone to find us a *calesa*, and took us home. My grateful father thanked the kind woman, scolded and spanked my brother, and admonished us not to jump from trams again. Fortunately, I was not seriously injured. Although we missed the rehearsal, we could still participate in the recital.

My ideal image of a piano recital contains a shiny black Steinway grand piano spotlighted on center stage of a town community center. Willow baskets of red roses, pink carnations, multicolored gladioli, green ferns, and baby's breath ringing the stage, anxious parents, siblings, grandparents in the audience, a music teacher with a wilted cattleya orchid corsage busily shepherding little boys and girls, all dressed in their Sunday best, squirming in their seats while waiting for their turn to play.

My first piano recital was none of the above. It took place in a small auditorium somewhere in South Manila in the middle of the war. There were no flowers on the tiny stage, only the piano and bench. My fingernails were trimmed, I was bathed, smelling of a *sampaguita* lei around my neck, long black hair separated into two braids tied with pink ribbons, wearing black patent shoes with white socks, and my best dress handed down from my sister Nena. However, my bandaged knees and chin and skinned elbows detracted from my appearance. I was the first, the shortest, and the youngest, seven years old. I was to play a short piece entitled "In May." I climbed six steps to the stage and walked to the center of the stage. Just as we had rehearsed a dozen times, I picked up the edges of my dress and took a low bow, my right knee bent. My knee rubbed against the Band-Aid and it hurt. I walked slowly to the piano bench and lifted myself slightly to sit on the hard wood, my short legs dangling. My hands started to sweat.

I positioned my hands over the piano keys, making certain that the fingers were on the first notes of my piece. The world of the audience vanished from my mind and my vision. I started hearing the tune even before I played the first notes. How many times I had played the piece from memory. Even in my sleep, I played the piece over and over, at the same time singing it to myself. When it was over, I was awakened from my reverie by the applause of relatives, friends, and strangers. I had performed my piece without skipping any notes and did not suffer from any stage fright. My piece was a success, and my brother's duet with Dulcy Aguinaldo, the granddaughter of the first President of the Philippines, was the highlight of the recital. They played magnifycently and received a standing ovation. Miss Luming beamed with pride afterward.

CHAPTER 12

Making a Living

BEFORE THE WAR, MY FATHER HAD WORKED AS A LAND SURVEYOR and also ran a company that produced blueprints for Manila city planners and builders (as well as some other small businesses). But the war made it dangerous for him to continue as a surveyor, as it had become unsafe to travel outside of Manila. There was not much need for blueprints. The town where my father was born, Meycauayan, Bulacan, was known for its goldsmiths and fine jewelry. My grandfather had wanted my father to follow in his footsteps as a goldsmith, but his premature death prevented my father from continuing in the same profession, so he ended up as a land surveyor. Now he used his knowledge about jewelry, learned as a child from his father, to start another business, reselling jewelry consigned to him by some of his acquaintances.

During World War II, many families became impoverished and had to sell their precious heirlooms and jewelry in order to survive. Many heads of families were unemployed and thus could not buy food and other goods for their children. My father had a reputation for honesty and fair dealing in those days when many were taking advantage of people's sudden poverty. His many friends and their friends trusted him to sell their jewelry for them at a fair price when times got hard during the Japanese occupation. Sometimes, he would buy the jewelry for himself, as an investment, whenever he had cash from the sale of his produce. The trick then was not to hold on to cash too long because of inflation. He was also partial to buying land whenever he made a profit from the sale of jewelry.

At the back of the house, a large room on the first floor opened to the *Estero Cegado*. It had very thick walls, and an exterior door indicated that this room had been used as a loading dock by the previous owners. This part of the house was dark and damp; the only light came from two small barred windows and a bare light bulb that dangled from the ceiling and cast shadows on the wall. We children pretended it was part of a pirates' lair, a secret hiding place. My father kept a tall iron safe for storing valuables that stood at the far end of the room.

Two women, middle-aged *Aling* Fidela and Virginia, did the actual selling for him. Aling Fidela had a consumptive husband and five children for whom she was the sole support. My father admired her hard work and strong business sense. Virginia was nicknamed Buntis, which means "the pregnant one," because she had a child every year. She worked to supplement her husband's income in order to support their ever-growing family.

The two women carried jewelry in their purses to prospective clients' homes, sometimes including very valuable gems or payments of large sums of money. Most of these clients were known to my father, who also trusted the two women implicitly. He took their word at how much the jewelry sold for.

One day, Virginia came running up the stairs, shouting that she had been robbed. The black leather purse she usually carried on her shoulder was gone. She was panting, and her maternity dress showed sweat marks as she reached the top of the stairs of the Arlegui house, her brown frizzy hair disheveled, her face flushed. She looked as if she were about to give birth.

"Calm down, Virginia," my father said, offering her a chair. "Sit down, and collect yourself. Now, tell me what happened."

"*Mang* Bino," Virginia began, "someone came from behind, grabbed my purse, and ran. I shouted for people to help me or call the police, but the thief was just too fast. They couldn't catch him. I am so sorry."

"I'm glad to see you were not hurt. Tell me, what jewelry were you carrying?"

"A sapphire ring and a pair of gold earrings."

"I think those belong to Mrs. de los Santos. I'll have to pay her out of my own funds."

"I feel awful. I'm really sorry, *Mang* Bino."

"Well, I don't think the police will ever recover the jewelry. But next time, please tuck your purse under your arm, like the way Fidela does. She has never been robbed, you know."

"I promise I will, from now on."

She was right. Virginia was never robbed again.

I always looked forward to going with my father when he went to the vault to unlock his safe. I listened sometimes to his conversation with the two women as he gave them rings, necklaces, bracelets, and earrings to sell. What I enjoyed the most was when he allowed Nena and me to touch the jewelry and explained things to us. When most girls my age were content to play with dolls, I was learning about cut, clarity, carat, and carbon defects in diamonds. I knew about karats in gold and could identify what was filigree work. My father also let me look through his loupe so that I could admire the precious stones in their beautiful gold settings. I was probably the only child of eight who could distinguish a real diamond from paste.

"Can I look at this diamond ring, Papá?"

"Here, hold it carefully. It's better to look at a diamond under a loupe. You can see better." He handed me what looked like a small magnifying glass and arranged it on top of the diamond. I had seen him and my uncles look through a loupe but did not know what they were called.

"Wow! It looks so big. What are those black dots?" I asked. I was surprised to see large black specks in the jewel. Without the loupe, they were not visible.

"Those are carbon defects. They are imperfections in the stone, and make the diamond less valuable. Remember these stones are mined. They come from the ground and from caves." He reached inside the safe and took out a box with lots of rings. "Take a look at this other solitaire. Do you see the difference?"

"This one looks so clear and brilliant. And it has no black dots. I'd like to have a diamond ring one day," I said as I fingered the beautiful solitaire.

My father looked at me and smiled. "You'll have to wait until you grow up."

Nena had followed me into the vault area. She picked up some earrings with different colored gems. "What do you call the red stone, Papá? It's as red as blood."

"That's a ruby." I thought my father enjoyed playing with the jewelry as much as I did. He seemed to be more relaxed when he was talking to us about the different gems.

"And the blue bracelet? What's that made of?" I asked.

My father took the bracelet from its case and placed it around my wrist. There were four identical perfect blue stones arranged in a row surrounded by tiny diamonds. The bracelet itself was made of gold. I lifted my left wrist and admired it next to the light. It was so beautiful. Then my father removed the bracelet from my wrist and returned it to its container.

"That's sapphire," he said.

"I love blue. I think from now on sapphire will be my favorite," I announced. "What's that green one? It looks like grass." I asked, touching a green ring inside a blue velvet box.

"That's an emerald. The darker they are, the prettier and more expensive they become." My father took out a pair of earrings and held them in his hands. "See this pair? They are cloudier than this dark green ring. They are both emeralds, but the darker one is more expensive because it has fewer imperfections and is not as common.

"I like the rubies," Nena said, grabbing a gold ring with a red stone. "They sparkle and are mysterious. Someday, can I have a ruby ring with matching earrings?"

"Perhaps when you are older, I'll give you some nice pieces of jewelry. But you have to take care of them. They are very valuable and easily lost." My father did keep his promise. I was given an antique sapphire bracelet and a matching ring on my eighteenth birthday. I still have them today.

We children mimicked my father and his jewelry business as we did everything he did. I enjoyed rolling the aluminum foil sheets from the inside of cigarette packs into balls and pretending they were gold or jewelry. We used to play "buy and sell" with them. We cut up paper, wrote peso amounts on them to simulate money, and used them as currency in our gold business. We copied every aspect of the business, down to the haggling, and imitating one of the salesperson's reactions to her being robbed. No guest to our house escaped without surrendering the foil from his cigarette box.

Many people found themselves doing things that they would ordinarily avoid to survive during the war. The lines between moral and wrong became more gray. This was true for the family of Nenita, Hiram's wife. Some years earlier, Nenita's younger sister, Marta, while out for a walk, was "kidnapped" by a neighborhood gangster who lived on Elizondo Street. That street was known as the place where all the petty thieves and pickpockets lived. She came home, a year later, with a child and husband. The gangster turned out to be a good son-in-law. He provided food for the family during the war when it was almost impossible to obtain. The family would not have survived without him, and so he finally won their acceptance.

Nenita herself had a difficult time after Hiram's disappearance, and their son Herman suffered from serious health problems. When Herman was just a few months old, he got very ill. I remember the anxious moments the older people in the house had when Herman's high fever wouldn't go down. I heard him cry all the time. The doctor came often, and there were lots of sleepless nights for everyone. It was much later when I found out he had suffered from polio. Not knowing much about the highly contagious disease, it was amazing none of us children caught it. Herman survived polio, but it left his left leg shrunken and crippled.

Nenita's beauty, youth, and uncertain marital status, since no one knew for sure whether her husband was dead or alive, created problems for my father. Men came to our house to talk business with my father, but soon returned as suitors to Nenita. One of the more persistent visitors was Mariano, a widower and business acquaintance of my father who had children older than Nenita. He often visited and talked to my father, but Nenita seemed to always be around whenever he came. I did not understand at first why he kept coming.

Then one day, we were in the dining room overlooking the kitchen and the river, at the back of the house on Arlegui Street, watching my oldest sister Fe bake a cake. The sweet smell of vanilla being beaten into the cake batter wafted over us. Fe, not yet sixteen, loved to bake cakes. My sister Nena and I waited for the special treat baking in the oven. The cook, who also worked as our laundress, was pressing our clothes. When I opened the door to our icebox to get a drink of cold water, I got a shock as usual from touching the door. Then I saw my nephew Herman, sitting on top of the dining table. The strap of his overall had slipped off his shoulder, and he was playing with the bottle of soy sauce. He had just turned two.

"What's Herman doing on the dining table? Look, he's poured soy sauce all over his body!" I said.

My father, who had just returned home, asked, "Where's his mother?"

The cook replied, "We don't know, sir. She hasn't returned home since going shopping this morning. But she left a note for you, sir."

I knew it was not good news when I saw the frown on my father's face after reading the note.

He crumpled it roughly and shouted, "Nenita has run away with Mariano. How can she do this to her husband, who may be dying or starving in the jungle at this moment?"

I could tell from my father's voice that he was very angry. I grabbed hold of Herman and led him away.

Fe cried, "But Mariano is old enough to be her father. How could she?"

My father ignored this and said, "From now on, this house is off limits to Nenita. Do you all understand? She is not to see her son ever again." As he left the dining room, he accidentally hit the dinner gong used to summon us for meals. It sounded a loud "bong," and the noise reverberated throughout the house.

Herman became the subject of a bitter custody battle between my father and Nenita. My father had greater financial resources and ultimately won the legal battle, but it dragged on for years during the war. He got custody of Herman and legally adopted him so that he became my brother instead of my nephew. Herman grew up spoiled by my father, who saw in him the son he had lost, pitied by everyone because of his polio and shriveled left leg, and abandoned by his mother, who soon started another family with Mariano.

Like his father, Herman did not like school. He also inherited his mother's addiction to gambling (Nenita had started playing mahjongg for high stakes every day). Many years later, after I had grown up and moved to Indiana in the United States, my brother Eddy encouraged Herman to visit me in Indiana, to interest him in going to college there. But Herman had only one interest at the time, to visit Las Vegas. When I was cleaning his room after his visit, I found two mementos: a worn deck of cards and a half-empty bottle of Kentucky Bourbon.

After my father died, Herman inherited the share of his estate that would have gone to his father Hiram. With his newly acquired financial independence, Herman had no need to work. He lived on a generous allowance that he spent on gambling and women. Herman started running around with an older woman who turned out to be a mobster's girlfriend. One day, I received a letter from Eddy, not a phone call nor a telegram, but a letter, informing me of Herman's death. He had been shot by an unknown assailant, and his murder was never solved. Everyone believed that the mobster did not want to share his girlfriend and had hired someone to kill Herman.

Herman's violent death upset me a great deal. I couldn't believe that someone I cared about, with whom I had played as a child, would be murdered. I remembered the little boy I used to carry, much too heavy and large for my age. He used to follow me around, demanding I play with him. I enjoyed the attention and preference he gave me, but there were times when I thought him a pest, an interloper. Although I didn't approve of how he chose to live his life, I was sorry to see it end the way it did.

CHAPTER 13
Tía Josefa

TÍA JOSEFA, MY FATHER'S SECOND OLDEST SISTER, lived with her husband some distance away from us. Because of the hardships of the war, we didn't see much of her. She had married Enrique, the brother of a famous lawyer. He wore dark rimmed glasses covering large, childlike eyes. He spoke in a soft, overly effusive manner. When we visited their house, he greeted me by calling me "this beautiful flower gracing our home." Even at a young age, I didn't trust him.

Inay called Enrique the failure of the family because his business ventures failed more often than they succeeded. *Inay* said that he complained so much about how their servants did things that my *Tía* Josefa was forced to do everything in the house.

"That's how Josefa got TB, from overwork, from having a husband like Enrique," *Inay* said. My aunt had suffered for many years with this sickness.

One day in 1943, when I was seven years old, *Inay* took my sister Nena and me to visit *Tía* Josefa in the hospital and say goodbye to her. She was at the San Juan de Dios Hospital, a tuberculosis sanitarium, and she was dying. I recognized the hospital from an earlier visit. We had been taken there once to get X-rayed, then called "fluoroscopy," to check whether our lungs were clear. The dark room, lit only by violet lights, made all the white-clad nurses and doctors appear surreal. Their hands and faces looked purple, frightening me and making me cry. An elderly nurse had to embrace me and murmur comforting words to get me to stop crying.

From the hospital corridor, I could hear sounds of coughing coming from various rooms. Strong smells of disinfectant and medicine permeated the beige hallway that led to patients' rooms. Occasionally, I heard medicine bottles clinking and glasses tinkling as orderlies pushed carts bearing them. People seemed to be rushing, and nobody paused to talk. I heard no laughter and saw no smiles.

It was all in sharp contrast to the children's hospital where I was taken when I was stricken with pneumonia a few years before. I remember the rush to the hospital on a bumpy *calesa* ride, bundled in a pink cotton blanket, cradled by our cook, *Aling* Nilda, who smelled of garlic on her hands and fish on her clothes. My legs stretched across the laps of *Aling* Nilda and Dr. Josef, our family physician, seated next to her. She had been interrupted during lunch preparation in order to take me to the hospital. I had come down with a very high fever, and Dr. Josef had deemed it necessary that I be hospitalized. *Inay* had followed in another *calesa*. The next morning, I woke up thinking I had died and was in heaven because I heard laughter and bouncing balls amid swaying palms under a cloudless blue sky. But my fever had broken, and what I heard was the laughter from doctors and nurses while on a break, playing tennis in the hospital courtyard.

We entered *Tía* Josefa's room at the end of a long corridor. I smelled more disinfectant as soon as I passed the doorway. She was reclining in bed, propped up on several pillows, staring out the open window. I had not seen her for months, and the change in her appearance surprised me. Her normally black hair, now braided singly and dangling onto her left shoulder, had turned white, blending with the white batiste nightgown that covered her thin body.

"I am so happy to see you, *Ate* Milia. And you brought the girls. How nice. But don't come near me."

She was obviously pleased to see us. She motioned us to sit on a cane chair in the opposite corner from her bed. There was only one chair, so Nena and I had to share.

"Go sit down over there in the corner by the window. I want to get a good look at you. My, you girls have grown." She smiled and eyed us from head to toe.

Tía Josefa started to cough as soon as she started talking. She looked apologetic as she covered her mouth with a handkerchief.

Inay looked worried. "Can I do something? Should I call the nurse?"

Tía Josefa said, "No, I'm all right. Perhaps just a sip of water." Nena and I watched her as she took a half-filled glass of water standing on a soaked napkin by her bedside table. I noticed a slight tremble in her hand.

We were not permitted to approach or kiss her. Normally, we would have kissed the back of her hand, which is sign of respect in the Philippines. I remember how affectionate she was when we used to visit her at her home. Her house sparkled, and her kitchen overflowed with good things to eat. I always looked forward to our visits to her home.

Nena said, "Hello, *Tía*." I did not say anything, just smiled and looked at her.

"Are you comfortable now? Is everyone treating you well?" *Inay* asked. During previous visits, *Inay* had fussed over her, fluffed her pillows, and arranged her blanket. This time, she didn't do any of these.

"I am all right, now. Thank you. I have my good and bad days." *Tía* Josefa's breathing got heavier, and she was wheezing. I could tell she was having problems talking.

She paused for a while and then continued. "Everyone has been wonderful. The nurses have been so kind. I have you and Bino [my father] to thank for this private room. You know Enrique could not have afforded this. We don't want to ask money from his sister again. They have already done so much for us."

"You shouldn't worry about money and expenses. Just get well. Here, we brought you some fruits. It's getting difficult to find them, but, luckily for all of us, Bino's fruit orchards are still producing." *Inay* laid down the small paper bag full of fruits on an adjoining table.

"Thank you so much. I enjoyed the mangoes you brought last time. I don't get to eat much fruit around here." *Tía* Josefa looked at the bag longingly. I heard a loud, piercing cough from the room next door.

Our conversation was interrupted by *Tío* Enrique's arrival. He opened the door with a bang that startled me. As he removed his Panama hat to wipe his perspiration, I noticed the balding head and large brown eyes hidden by round sunglasses. He hesitated in the doorway, like a stranger waiting for permission to enter.

Staying as far away from the bed as he could, he glanced at us and removed his glasses and wiped his brows. "Do you know how long it took me to get here? One and a half hours! It's getting very difficult to find a *calesa,* and I had to walk the last mile to get here. I may not be able to visit you as often as you'd like me to come."

My aunt said, "Oh, don't worry about it. I don't want you to get tired. You don't have to come every day. I do get lots of visits from my sister Emilia and my brothers."

"Well, how are you, Sefa?"

"I am feeling a little weak today. And you? How are things at home? The children?" My aunt had started coughing again. She clasped her chest and was unable to keep speaking. *Tío* Enrique started talking over her coughing.

"Oh, the children are all right. But I'm not happy with the girl who irons my clothes. She doesn't do as good a job as you used to do. And she's a very bad cook. She overcooks everything." He frowned as he spoke. He had returned his handkerchief to his pants pocket.

"If you send her here, I can tell her how to iron your shirts and cook your vegetables the way you like them. I'm sorry I'm not home to do those things for you." Her voice sounded feeble. She took another sip of water. "How long can you stay today?" she asked.

I began to fidget on the chair I shared with Nena. Nena was trying to slowly push me out of the chair, and I was staying put. I was relieved to see that *Inay* did not notice what Nena and I were doing. *Inay* was glaring at her brother-in-law. But she did not say anything.

Tío Enrique answered, "Not long. In fact, I should be going now. I want to make sure I can find a *calesa* to take me home."

He turned toward the sink and washed his hands vigorously with the disinfectant. Without saying goodbye, he was out of the room and gone. I saw tears in my *Tía* Josefa's eyes and fury in my *Tía* Emilia's.

Tía Josefa did not live long after that visit. She died in her sleep and was buried in the family plot. I did not attend her funeral, but I heard from *Inay* that *Tío* Enrique cried the loudest of everyone.

CHAPTER 14

Another New Home

FROM THE BEGINNING OF THE JAPANESE OCCUPATION, we would see wooden plaques containing Japanese characters appear on buildings and homes. This was how people discovered their property was being confiscated by the Japanese. A vertical rectangular wooden plaque with painted Japanese characters in white, measuring approximately one by two feet, would be nailed on their doors. Since I couldn't read Japanese, I didn't know exactly what it said, but the characters apparently meant something like "Property of the Japanese Imperial Government." That sign, which started appearing more frequently on doors as the war neared its end, always brought fear and panic to the occupants. Housing had become tight in Manila, and it was not easy to find another place to live.

One day, a Japanese officer who was a frequent visitor to our house came to announce that the Japanese Army was taking over our house to billet their officers. My father had befriended some Japanese officers with the view of preventing the confiscation of our house. Lt. Fukuda was one of them, and he was attracted to my oldest sister Fe and often came to visit. He was very courteous, unlike the many soldiers we encountered who demanded we bow to them or else would slap our faces. He wore a long, sharp sword, sheathed in a shiny scabbard, that he always removed and placed against a table before sitting. My brother Vic used to scare my nephew Herman by saying that if he misbehaved, Lt. Fukuda would castrate him with his sword.

Since Lt. Fukuda had given us advance warning, we were not surprised when the much-feared plaque appeared on the front door of the Arlegui house. Other officers also came to our house in order to apologize profusely. No one could do anything about the confiscation, but my father was given enough time to locate another house for us before we had to vacate. He rented a two-story house on Vision Street back in the neighborhood where we were all born, a block away from where *Inay* lived.

After the spaciousness of Arlegui Street, the rented house at 529 Vision Street seemed gloomy and tiny. We crowded into its small bedrooms upstairs, and every inch of space downstairs was covered with our furniture. Vision was not a street; it was an alley, a narrow unpaved road with two adjacent sewage ditches that we called "canals." There was always sewage water sitting in these canals. The alley was filled with clouds of mosquitoes and the stench of sewage. There was only room for one car or *calesa* to pass. Since nobody owned a car during the war, the alley was our playground. The alley ended at the tall walls of the Chinese General Hospital.

Our North Manila neighborhood near the Cementerio del Norte

One nice thing about this house was its backyard. We could plant vegetables and raise chickens. At that time, our meals had been reduced to rice and boiled *kangkong*, native spinach. Soon after moving into the house on Vision Street, other green vegetables and chicken started appearing on our plates.

We did not stay long in the yellow house on Vision Street, perhaps half a year. A small house on the other side of the street from our rented house became available for sale when the father of the household became seriously ill and that family decided to move in with relatives in the countryside. My father took the opportunity to buy a house not far from the neighborhood where most of his brothers and sisters lived and where we had lived as small children. We moved into our fifth house at 534 Vision before the war ended.

The pink wooden chalet, whose square footage was smaller than the living room in our Arlegui house, had only three bedrooms of varying sizes. The largest was shared by Nena and me and the two maids, Luisa and Meneng. My father and brother Eddy occupied the middle room. My oldest sister Fe was given the smallest bedroom, just enough to hold a twin bed and a dresser, which she did not have to share with anyone.

Nena's and my bedroom was originally painted yellow but was repainted blue later on. You entered it through double doors. It had two large corner windows, iron-barred to prevent burglars from entering the house. Large sliding wood windows on tracks, with upper panels decorated with small squares of translucent mother-of-pearl shell, provided privacy and protection from the rain. We could not afford to curtain the windows during the war, other than covering them with black cloths. Any fabric available was used for clothing, not a luxury item such as curtains.

The original long living room was divided into a dining room and a bedroom for the younger boys: Vic, Paking, and Herman. A veranda that was open to the elements but iron-barred on two sides became our living room. It was also the entry to the house. Every time it rained, the living room got soaked, so we had bamboo shutters installed over the windows. The piano, Chinese rug, and half of our rattan furniture from the Arlegui house barely fit into our new living room. My father gave the other half of our living room furniture to his friend, Don Juan, a fellow Mason, who had lost all his possessions. It turned out Don Juan was really John Schultz, a German Jew.

The ten of us shared one bathroom with only a shower, a sink, and a toilet. There was no hot water. We took cold showers or boiled water that we mixed with cold water to pour over our bodies. During the hot summer months, a cold shower was a welcome treat, but during December, we had to boil the water for bathing.

Towards the back of the house, reached by going down eight steps, was a large covered area, open on one side to rain and wind, that served as the kitchen and maids' workroom. The previous owners, who had also had a large family, ate their meals down here. But we decided to eat upstairs inside the house. Luisa cooked below and brought the food upstairs for our meals. She also washed our clothes, while Meneng, our servant from Iloilo, cleaned the house and helped us with daily tasks.

At night, we used mosquito nets to protect us from the large swarms of insects which shared the house with us. The windows were not screened, so all kinds of insects flew in and out of the house at will. In addition to the flying insects, the ceiling was home to the geckos, little beige native lizards, about six inches long with long tails, that ate the insects. Sometimes the geckos would lose their footing and fall on me as I lay in bed. The geckos felt cold. They never bit me, and were likely just as frightened as I was so that we ended up jumping at the same time. Whenever I had problems sleeping, I used to watch them move slowly around the ceiling, making a little "tick, tick" noise that was barely audible. Sometimes, they remained anchored frozen near the light for hours.

The house resembled a Scout encampment because the mosquito nets looked like tents. Often, the bare bulbs hanging from the ceiling attracted a motley swarm of flying insects at night. My father would instruct Meneng to stand on a chair holding a white basin half-filled with water underneath the light source. Soon, the flying insects, attracted by the reflected light, turned to the water-filled basin, drowning in the process.

Underneath the house was the partially exposed, latticed-walled basement that we used as a play area. We would go down every morning to roller skate on its cement floor. It was a lot of fun chasing each other on roller skates as we went around the basement. The old metal skates, tightened by keys to fit different shoe sizes when new, now were held together by a piece of twine. Nena and I shared a pair of roller skates so I became an expert on skating on one foot while she used the other half of the pair.

When the rainy season came, water started filling the outer edges of the basement. We continued to skate on the dry part. A sump pump took out most of the water, but as we got deeper into the rainy season, the pump could no longer remove the water fast enough. We had to move our games to the front yard, where a large mango tree stood. I learned to climb this tree, but fear prevented me from scaling it all the way to the top like my brothers. Even though it bore fruit, we were not fast enough to pick them because neighborhood kids got to them first. Many flowering bushes, such as poinsettia and red hibiscus, grew along the front fence, providing privacy. An avocado tree that bore no fruit stood outside our front window. Dark red bougainvillea framed the front windows where we hung star-shaped paper lanterns, lit by a single bulb, at Christmas time.

The previous owners had fenced the area below my bedroom window. My father kept some chickens and a small black pig there. I was not happy with the smell coming from the yard below where we kept the animals. But I did not complain when the pig was butchered and the chickens slaughtered so that we could have meat during the war. The pig was an ordinary pig, not very large, black with some white on his head, and a long snout. He wallowed in mud just below our bedroom and was a squealer. I don't remember how we got him. Most likely, he was brought to us by one of my father's caretakers. I used to watch him frolic and snort, quite unaware of the feast he would offer us. I had never seen a pig slaughtered before. It was horrible. I could not forget the sight of blood spurting from the pig and the squeal he gave. I thought it was the loudest, most tortured scream I had ever heard. To this day, I understand where the phrase "you are squealing like a pig" originated.

Nena and I slept on two narrow cane beds, which occasionally had bedbugs so that they had to be taken outside and fumigated with a chemical that I believe was DDT. After the war, DDT was routinely sprayed around the house against mosquitoes and on the beds. I could tell we had bedbugs whenever I developed red, itchy welts on my bottom. Also, I learned to recognize the black bloodsucking bedbugs underneath the woven cane. They doubled in size after having bitten me. When the weather was too hot for a mattress, a tatami-style mat covered the bed instead. I used three pillows and an occasional top sheet when the nights got cold in December.

One day, when opening my chest of drawers, I saw three tiny black baby mice, all huddled together, sound asleep on top of shredded paper and tiny wood shavings. I was glad I never saw the mother. Meneng had to take the drawers outside and clean them to get rid of the nest and its residents. I was told to try to be neater and not to eat in the bedroom.

After we moved to Vision Street, Miss Luming could no longer give us piano lessons due to the distance. My father found another piano teacher in our new neighborhood. Miss Romero was a Spaniard who also gave Spanish lessons. After our piano lessons, she would write Spanish sentences on our little blackboard that she asked us to read and translate.

It was 1944, and the American bombing of Manila began to interfere with our piano lessons, as well as every other part of our lives. Hearing air raid sirens again meant fear of being bombed. But this time, we were being bombed by our friends. At least the Americans tried to hit only Japanese, not civilian, targets, but many innocent civilians still got killed. Windows had to be covered with black cloths, and lights had to be extinguished at night when the sirens sounded. Often, electricity was cut so that we lived by candlelight.

With the bombing of Manila, the few schools not taken over by the Japanese Army had to be closed again. It had become too dangerous for children to walk outside and go to school. I did not resume my education again until after the war, when I was nine and had to start in second grade again.

Miss Romero was terrified of bombs. We spent more time in our air-raid shelter under the stairs than receiving piano lessons from her. It was a very small space with a narrow wooden bench, but it served adequately as an air-raid shelter. I don't think Miss Romero would have come to our house to teach us piano had our air-raid shelter not passed her inspection. She often talked about the shrapnel that fell in the house she shared with her mother, missing her mother by an inch. "*Por eso, kasing laki ng tabako*" (therefore, it was as big as a cigar), she said in a mixture of Tagalog and Spanish, referring to the size of the shrapnel.

In her forties like Miss Luming, Miss Romero was fair and pretty. While both women had long brown hair, Miss Romero twisted her hair into a bun on top of her head, giving an appearance of a halo. She spoke Tagalog haltingly, not always sure of her words. But both teachers were wonderful pianists. We feared Miss Luming, while we could twist Miss Romero around our little fingers. We could tell her what she could assign us. If we didn't want to learn any particular Czerny exercise piece, we told her so, and she acquiesced. But I don't remember anything she taught me.

The only Spanish I remember from Miss Romero's lessons are these two sentences. "*La manzana es una fruta*": The apple is a fruit. "*La quinina es una medicina*": Quinine is a medicine. We continued our piano and Spanish lessons with Miss Romero until she found it too dangerous to come to our house. We never heard from Miss Romero again. We weren't even sure if she survived the liberation, during which one in seven Manila residents was killed.

During this time, I developed a fear of fire. A house in the neighborhood, about a block away, had caught fire. I was not permitted to join the bystanders looking at the fire; I could only watch the burning inferno from our kitchen window. Even though I could hear the wailing sirens from the fire trucks and knew they were putting out the fire, the billowing flames and smoke, first intense black, then ash gray, scared me to death. I heard later that the people living in the house lost everything they owned. Every night after that, I prepared my escape in case of fire. I bundled all my clothes and toys inside a sheet and tied all the corners together so they would be easy to carry in case of fire.

As time went on, it seemed as if the American pilots no longer stopped for sleep or food. It was one continuous bombing raid after the other. We left the black cloths that covered all the windows permanently on. Electricity was cut off. We ate and read by candlelight. The drone of the airplanes and the resulting noise from the exploding bombs prevented me from sleeping. It was no longer safe to be out in the streets. Food became scarcer. There was no more meat or chicken available. We were lucky to have had a small vegetable garden, but soon I got tired of eating soupy rice with *kangkong* every day.

CHAPTER 15

My Family's Darkest Day

IT WAS VERY COMMON FOR FILIPINO MEN TO BE SEIZED IN THEIR HOMES and taken by Japanese soldiers to Fort Santiago, a prison built by the Spaniards in Intramuros, the old Spanish walled city near the harbor. No reason was given for their arrest, and they were often never heard from again.

From time to time, the Japanese would line up all men in a neighborhood, and another man with his head covered by a paper bag, holes cut out for his eyes and nose, would point out men from the line-up he thought were guerrilla sympathizers. The presumed guerrillas would then be taken, imprisoned, or executed. This was the dreaded *zona*; the word meant zone, but it became a synonym for the rounding up of neighborhood men. Literally anyone with a grudge against or envious of his neighbor could accuse him of being a spy, and that would be the end of that person.

Trying to remain on good terms with the Japanese was a common tactic used by many Filipinos to protect their families. However, I later learned my father had another motive for his seemingly friendly relations with local Japanese officers, as a cover for his relations with the Filipino resistance. As a very young girl, I was not told about all of my father's activities at the time. I do remember seeing a lot of different men coming to our house at night, conferring in hushed tones with my father and receiving money from him. These visits continued after our move to Vision

Street. After the war, when I was older, I learned that some of these men were caretakers on my father's land outside Manila and that they were all guerrillas opposing the Japanese regime. During the early part of the war, my father occasionally made surveying trips that served a dual purpose. All of these were very risky undertakings for my father. Everything had to be done surreptitiously because neighbors spied on neighbors.

The darkest day of the war came for us when one day, two Japanese soldiers in a small brown car pulled up in front of our house on Vision Street. They climbed up the eight steps to our main door, rang the bell, and asked for my father in halting Tagalog. They presented my father with a summons to appear at Army Headquarters: our own house on Arlegui Street!

The appearance of the two soldiers created quite a stir in the neighborhood and fear in our house. My father didn't know what they wanted from him. For the first time, I saw fear in his eyes. Perspiration drenched his worn-out shirt, dripped down his face and neck, and covered the palms of his hands as he said goodbye and kissed us.

"Don't wait up for me. I'll be back, probably quite late," were his parting words.

"Goodbye, Papá," we shouted, holding back our tears. We had heard enough about arrests and torture. We were worried he might not come back. Nena and I started to cry. The older ones tried to calm us down but to no avail.

Finally, Fe said, "You can cry as much as you want, but that will not bring Papá back any sooner. Why don't you kids play or do something."

Nena and I played with our dolls. It was very difficult to get enthusiastic about dolls when you were worried about your only parent not coming back. Then, we thought having friends over might distract us. We asked some neighborhood children, Loreto and Pilar, to come to our house and play with us. They were as curious as their parents. They all wanted to know where my father was being taken. We told them as much as we knew. They were sympathetic and kind, and related similar incidents that happened to their relatives with happy endings.

Hours passed. We kept looking out of the window to keep watch for my father. Then, at the entrance to Vision Street, we saw a familiar figure, hatless, wearing a white polo shirt and khaki pants, walking toward us.

Shouts of "Papá! Papá!" echoed throughout the alley.

Neighbors looked out of their windows and smiled. We were all over my father before he could climb our stairs and enter the house.

"You came back! Thank God!" we cried. "Tell us what happened."

He told us of his apprehension when he was taken to Army headquarters. He really thought he was being arrested and imprisoned. Earlier, he had received word that one of his farm caretakers had been arrested on charges of being a guerrilla. He was concerned that if tortured, the man might have talked. But then he saw Lt. Fukuda, who greeted him with a smile.

"Thank goodness! When I saw Lt. Fukuda smiling at me, I realized I wasn't even being arrested!" he said.

Paking's curiosity was piqued. "So, what happened then?"

"Do you know what they wanted with me? They were giving me back our house! Our house on Arlegui Street is now ours again," my father shouted. His voice tended to get loud when he got excited. I was sure our neighbors could hear him too.

"I wonder why they are giving us back our house at this time," Eddy said.

"I don't really know. But I think something is up. I saw soldiers hurriedly packing papers into boxes, and boxes were being loaded onto trucks parked outside. The house was being emptied of furniture and equipment. The soldiers followed one another as they loaded everything into vans and trucks, looking like ants carrying food to their nest." My father broke into a smile.

"Wow! I still can't believe it," said Vic.

"The house is ours again. The interior looks in good shape. The Japanese have not damaged the house. I am so grateful I wasn't arrested and we are all together again."

"When do we move back?" asked Eddy.

"I don't know. We'll have to wait and see. Somehow, I feel more secure living here than in Arlegui. That house is too near important government buildings," my father replied.

I never saw my father cry, but I thought I saw tears forming around his eyes. It reminded me of the day *Kapitan* Lauria told us about Hiram and the Death March. I could see relief all over his face. Nena and I were silent as my father talked. We each held on tightly to his hands. I thanked God for giving us back our father.

As I found out later, the Japanese High Command decided to retreat to South Manila across the Pasig River and defend their positions there. They were going to fight for the port of Manila and Intramuros. They brought enough food and ammunitions for a long siege. With this plan, the house on Arlegui Street had to be abandoned.

The Japanese Army moved men and material across the Quezon Boulevard Bridge as explosives and bomb fuses were being installed underneath. Other bridges connecting North and South Manila were also mined. After the Japanese soldiers and equipment had crossed Pasig River, to take up positions in the government office buildings across the river, the Commander of the Army gave the signal to blow up the bridges. The explosion rocked the center of Manila. The sound could be heard several kilometers away. Windows were blown out, nearby civilians killed, and small fires started near where the bridges were located.

My father's intuition about the location of the Arlegui house was accurate. Luckily for us, the house suffered only minor damage when the Quezon Boulevard Bridge was destroyed by the Japanese. But many nearby residents were killed by shrapnel and the resulting fire. They could not abandon their burning homes because the Japanese soldiers started shooting at the fleeing civilians.

This turned out to be only the beginning of the month-long siege now called the battle of Manila.

CHAPTER 16

The Liberation of Manila

As THE AMERICAN BOMBING OF MANILA BECAME MORE INTENSE so did the reports of Japanese cruelty toward Filipino civilians. The Japanese had assumed after the occupation of the Philippines that, being Asians, the Filipinos would embrace the Japanese regime, as many other Asian countries had. But despite the promise of an earlier independence for the Philippines, the Japanese could not persuade the Filipino population to change their allegiance from the Americans to the Japanese.

Food became even more scarce. *Copra*, the dried-up coconut meat used for fuel, became one of our food staples. We discovered that putting copra over live embers moistened the coconut and made it tasty. I loved its juicy flavor that gave me instant energy. I always seemed to have a stomachache after eating copra, but I still ate mounds of it. There was nothing else to eat.

I developed open sores on my legs again, much bigger than the ones I had when I was very young. My father said they were due to malnutrition and the lack of proper medication to treat them. He warned me frequently not to scratch the open wound lest I spread the infection and make it worse. I tried, but at night, I sometimes scratched the open wounds in my sleep. They were so itchy. I sometimes just scratched the perimeter of the wound, but eventually, I would touch the open sore, making it bleed and sting. Every morning, we would clean our wounds with soap and warm water. They were left open to dry. I still have scars on my legs today from these wounds.

One punishment the Japanese inflicted on the civilian population was to withhold all shipments of cloth to the Philippines. We all ended up with tattered clothing. I was down to three torn and often-mended dresses. Unfortunately, I tore my dresses as fast as they could be mended. Age, washing, and mending had weakened the cotton fabric of the dresses. Some of the holes got so large that they could no longer be mended. I felt lucky that I did not have to go to school in my shabby clothing.

My pride and joy, my red brocade satin Chinese slippers, also became tattered. The slippers, frequently mended in front, began to resemble a crocodile's snout. No amount of sewing could attach the front panel to the bottom. I cried when we finally had to throw them out. There were no replacement slippers available, so I had to walk barefoot inside the house. Outdoors, I either wore others' old wooden shoes or my old, outgrown leather shoes, which had been cut at the back so they would still fit me as my feet grew.

I passed by a mirror one day and saw a barefoot, frowning girl with sores on her legs and ribs visible through the large holes in her too-short dress. It took me a while to realize it was my own reflection.

Towards the end of 1944, rumors of an American landing on Philippine soil were passed from house to house in our neighborhood. Everyone was terrified. My father did not talk to us about his fear for his life, but I could see it in his eyes. He no longer left the house. He warned us not to talk to strangers or outsiders and to stay and play indoors.

Not until two former caretakers of my father's land came to our house one night did my father get the actual news that the American forces had indeed landed in Lingayen, about 200 kilometers north of Manila. The guerrilla unit of these two men had joined forces with the Americans, who had issued orders to demolish bridges and blow up supply dumps.

It turned out that there was a huge network of underground guerrillas, consisting of Filipinos sympathetic to the Americans and former soldiers and officers, who hid in the mountains with their weapons rather than surrender to the Japanese. They formed loose units all over the country, especially in the southern islands. The Japanese Army was never able to penetrate and conquer the whole country because of the Philippine geography of 11,000 miles of coastline as well as jungles, mountains, and the absence of roads made much of the country inaccessible.

These Filipinos, who stayed mainly in the mountains and inside the jungles, were never seen by the Japanese. They provided information on Japanese troop movement and location of ammunition. They spent the war years sending information regarding the location of fuel dumps, guns, and troop movements. They watched from beaches, sending out radio information on ships and ship movements to the American command in Australia. This information turned out to be very valuable during the American landings at Leyte and Lingayen. Were it not for these guerrillas, American pilots would not have learned of camouflaged air bases, secret headquarters, and ammunition dumps. The guerrillas hid downed American pilots from the Japanese. Without their help, the American forces would have suffered more casualties when they recaptured the Philippines.

It was because of his involvement with the guerrillas that my father had seemed so nervous at the end, when the Japanese were rounding up anyone on the smallest suspicion. My father learned of the American landing in Lingayen when the guerrillas he had supported came to our house. They wanted to reassure him. They gave him Chiclets and Hershey chocolate bars, proof of the Americans' nearby presence. He was sworn to secrecy and promised not to reveal any of this information to anyone. He did not tell us about it until after the Americans came to Manila. Then we got to eat the mouth-watering chocolate, such delicious food as I had not tasted in years.

We were in the Vision house when the American forces finally liberated our section of Manila on February 4, 1945. Unknown to us, an American unit had passed near our house the previous night in order to free about 4,000 prisoners of war, mostly American civilians, on the campus of Santo Tomás University. Somehow, I was not aware that not more than six blocks from our house, prisoners of war were held captive. They were near death because of disease and starvation when the Americans freed them.

We did not hear the noise of the tanks and other armored vehicles carrying the troops as they triumphantly rode down the streets of Manila. It was my cousin Cesar, who lived behind us on Dimasalang Street, who ran to our house shouting, "The Americans are coming! They are here!"

We dropped everything we were doing and ran down the narrow path behind our house, a short cut to Dimasalang Street. I usually walked very slowly on this path, checking carefully from side to side, because Vic had found several small snakes here among the tall grasses and weeds. He held them up wound around a stick to scare us. This time, I did not fear the snakes. I ran through the weeds as fast as my legs could carry me.

I heard the rumble of moving vehicles as I approached the street. It was my first sight of American soldiers. The victors were slowly parading before the cheering crowd. They were young, perhaps Eddy's age, very light in complexion but with sunburned red skin and short-cropped sandy hair, smiling and waving. They were seated inside and atop tanks, brown trucks, and strange-looking vehicles that I later learned were called "jeeps." They held their guns in one hand and waved with the other.

People were lined up three deep on the street when we arrived. Everyone was shouting, "Victory, Joe," and forming the "V" sign with their middle and second fingers. The noise from the cheers was deafening. From farther away, it had sounded like the waves breaking against the sea wall of Manila Bay.

When I saw that many people were giving the soldiers something to drink, I ran back to the house and grabbed a pitcher of Eddy's eggnog and a clean glass. My brother Eddy, due to his illness, took a glass of fresh eggnog every day, whenever we could get eggs and milk.

I offered a glass of eggnog to a blond GI sitting atop a tank. He climbed down, drank the eggnog, thanked me, patted me on the head, and gave me a Philippine peso stamped with the word VICTORY on one side. It was my first glimpse of the new currency. I kept that peso as a souvenir for a long time. People eventually had to turn in their old currency and have it stamped with VICTORY to be valid.

The sound of gunshots interrupted the joy and excitement. Everyone ran for cover. We had to seek refuge in my uncle's house but kept watch from a second floor window. The soldiers got back inside their tanks and trucks with guns and rifles cocked. They cornered a small platoon of surprised Japanese soldiers and captured them. It was a rare sight to find Japanese soldiers surrendering. Most of them fought to the death rather than get caught alive. We were just glad not to have witnessed any street fighting.

Everyone in the neighborhood was elated that day, hugging and laughing. That evening, as we sat down to eat our meager portions of food under candlelight, even my father, who never prayed, offered thanks to God that the war was over. We had survived the war. It was hard to believe that the war was over, at least for us.

After the American soldiers' entry into Manila, the Filipino looters followed. They entered a Japanese garrison in La Loma and started stealing everything the Japanese had abandoned. I saw grown men rolling barrels of oil along the street. Men, women, and children ran with boxes of food and clothing. Somehow, some people believed the war had made it all right for people to steal, as long as it was from the enemy.

From my bedroom window, I could see American soldiers setting up their hammocks in between tanks on our little street for the night. From the same windows during the day, I saw and heard artillery and cannons fired, directed at the retreating Japanese defending South Manila. What we did not know at the time was that Filipino civilians were also being killed.

One night, the soldiers did not set up their hammocks. They were not going to sleep. Instead, they started firing their big guns nonstop. Their target: Intramuros and South Manila across the river. The Japanese were not surrendering. Orders were given to pound them with mortar day and night. The sound was deafening. To know that these cannons were being fired to kill people and destroy buildings scared me.

I cried, "When will this end? I can't sleep!"

"Katinka," my father said, "Stop complaining. It's only noise. Cover your ears with cotton. You should think of the people who are on the receiving end of these guns. There are probably many dead on the other side of the river. Just think how lucky we are."

"I wouldn't want to be in their shoes," Vic said. I agreed with him and was sorry I had complained.

CHAPTER 17

Our Cousins, The von Giese Family

WE WERE STILL CELEBRATING THE ARRIVAL of the American forces into Manila in February 1945 when my father brought home a family of five one evening: a couple and their three daughters. They looked bedraggled and war-torn. The von Giese family had arrived at our house on Vision Street.

Although they looked nothing like us, the mother Patricia was my first cousin on my mother's side, the daughter of my mother's older sister. She was a beautiful, slender woman, in her late thirties, with clear gray eyes and short curly brown hair. She hugged me and gave me a short kiss. I couldn't remove my gaze from her because she looked so much like my mother, as I remembered her from her photographs.

Patricia spoke Spanish to us and was quite surprised to discover that we did not speak nor understand Spanish. My mother's grandparents had originally come from Madrid, Spain. They had objected to my mother marrying my father, resulting in estrangement between the two families. Now, in her family's time of need, my mother's niece remembered she had cousins living in North Manila.

Her husband was a German named Hans von Giese. He was a tall, thin, light-complexioned man, with receding hairline and a long hooked nose. He extended his long bony hands to shake mine. He looked ill at ease after the shock of their narrow escape.

We stared at three thin, tall identical-looking girls, with long scraggly blonde hair, haggard blue-gray eyes, and dirty white freckled faces. Blood had dried on their bony knees and stained parts of their dresses. Their names were Josephine, Jocelyn, and Janice, ages twelve, eleven, and ten. They had no clothes except those on their backs. The von Giese girls looked around our overcrowded house on Vision Street, the narrow unmade beds set up adjoining the dining room, the heavily-scratched round oak dining table that accommodated diners in shifts. They did not say anything.

The von Giese family had just escaped from the Ermita district in South Manila. They had a beautiful house in one of the most elegant areas. I remember the Ermita district. It was an upper-class residential area quite unlike ours. The streets, lined with palm trees and flowering acacias, were wide and paved with sidewalks. Architect-designed mansions, with automatic gates and tall stone fences topped by broken glass, were set back behind wide expanses of grass and landscaped gardens. It was the district where only rich Filipinos and foreigners resided.

Just before the war, my brothers, sister, and I developed severe cases of whooping cough. Dr. Josef, our family physician, recommended "sea air" to soothe our itchy throats and calm our hacking coughs. My father rented a pink house in Ermita, one of two identical rental houses, a block from Dewey Boulevard and the stone break wall over Manila Bay.

After the Japanese invasion, Dewey Boulevard received a name change, becoming Roxas Boulevard, after the first president of the Philippine Republic. All streets and buildings named after Americans were renamed by the Japanese authorities. The wide boulevard, once flanked by expanses of lawn and swaying palm trees, was stripped of trees and converted to an airstrip by the Japanese. This was the part of Manila that suffered the most under the American siege.

Patricia told us of their escape from Ermita, pausing often to sob. She began, "We had just returned from the cemetery, visiting my mother's grave, when a colleague of Hans, Thomas, intercepted us before we got home. He had already taken his family to safety when he saw us. He told us not to go home, not even take anything from home since the Japanese had decided to burn the area."

She stopped, took a sip of water, and continued, "They had started shooting at people escaping from the fire. It was horrible. Thomas literally dragged all five of us into his back yard. We waited until it got dark. There was gunfire all around us. Flames were leapfrogging across the street, burning everything along its way. You can imagine the horror. Oh, my poor girls, to have witnessed these atrocities. We were one step ahead of the flames and the Japanese soldiers."

"How did you cross the river?" asked my father.

"Thomas led us to a tunnel that some guerrillas had dug. It was not very long, but it went below the street and provided safety from the roaming soldiers above. We had to crawl on our hands and knees. It was dark and wet."

Patricia stopped talking. She looked at her daughters and touched their hands as she continued. "The girls were bleeding and crying. We finally saw the end of the tunnel. It ended at the river where a *banca*, small boat like a canoe, was tied to a tree. We paddled quietly across the Pasig River, thankful for the moonless night, amid gunfire from both sides of the river. All the bridges on the Pasig River had been bombed and destroyed. The Americans were shelling the Japanese positions in South Manila. The Japanese retaliated by torching the houses and killing the fleeing occupants. It was so terrible."

She started to cry, wiping her tears with a handkerchief.

"Take your time," my father said.

"We saw several people being killed, shot while they were running. All I could think was 'Thank God it's not us!' And those voices of people moaning and dying. I shall never forget them. I kept praying to God that our ordeal would end. I am so thankful we are all alive!"

"I'm glad you are all safe," my father said.

"What happened to Thomas?" we asked.

"That brave man. He decided to go back and save some more people."

"I hope he survives," my brother Eddy said.

We cried as Patricia told their story. We thanked God they were spared and that we did not suffer what they had suffered.

The Battle of Manila

By 1945, the Americans held the upper hand in the Pacific and the Philippines was in the process of being liberated. General Douglas MacArthur, who was forced out of the Philippines in 1941, was leading the charge to liberate the city of Manila. The Americans wished to try and spare the civilian population of the city, but large scale devastation from the battle couldn't be avoided.

As the Japanese forces were coming under increased fire, it was clear that they would lose. In response to this, they retaliated against the civilian population of Manila, which included massacres, violent mutilations, and rape. As a result of this outpouring of Japanese rage and the assault by the Americans to recapture the city, Manila was reduced to rubble. Only Warsaw in Poland suffered more damage than the Philippine capital.

My father generously offered sanctuary to these previously-unknown relatives. "We'll be a little bit crowded and uncomfortable, but I think we'll manage. Patricia, you and Hans and the children can use my bedroom. I am afraid the girls will have to sleep on the floor since there's only one bed there," my father said.

"It will be fine, Uncle. We are just grateful to have a roof over our heads after our ordeal," Patricia said.

My father continued, "We should not have problems with clothes for you and your girls. Fe, Nena, and Katinka's clothes should fit all of you. But Hans is just too tall. We'll find something for him tomorrow."

He turned to Luisa, who was watching. "Please serve them some dinner."

"Sir, we finished the chicken."

"Why don't you make some rice and cook some eggs. Do we still have eggs?"

"Only two, sir. But I can make an omelet with some leftover vegetables."

"That will be fine."

Food had been scarce, and we often had only rice and vegetables. An occasional chicken was a special treat. The eggs were for my oldest brother Eddy's eggnog. Fresh fruits, vegetables, milk, and eggs were required for his diet.

Starting that night, my father slept in Fe's room. Fe moved in with Nena and me, taking over my bed. I slept on the floor with the two maids. Brothers Eddy and Vic slept on the narrow beds while brother Paking and nephew Herman slept on the floor next to the dining table.

During the night, I was awakened by sobbing from the next room. Even though they were close relatives, I did not know them, but I felt so sorry for what they had been through, what they had lost. I repeated my prayer of thanks.

The von Giese girls did not talk much. They did not speak Tagalog, only Spanish and English. My father communicated with them in Spanish.

Eventually, the girls joined us on the floor in our games with stones and tamarind seeds. They easily understood us and learned the game. Nena and I were happy to have girls near our age to play with. We tried to make them feel welcome. They were nice to us, and we all got along well together, despite the crowded situation. It took a lot of patience on everyone's part to enable fifteen people to share one bathroom and eat meager servings of unappetizing food. That's one of the good things war did for people. You ate whatever food was served on the table because there might not be any next time. You also learned to be patient and to not complain too much.

The von Giese girls were the first Caucasian girls I ever played with. Until then, the only blond hair I had seen was on our dolls or at a distance when we were in Ermita and saw residents passing by. We introduced the girls to native games they had never played before. They had lived in Manila all their lives and yet had never really mixed with Filipinos. Such was the social environment in South Manila where they grew up. They were raised by Chinese *amahs* (nannies) and had attended only private Catholic schools ran by foreign nuns.

During our one-month stay in Ermita before the war, Isabel would walk us to the park across Dewey Boulevard where we would play and take picnics while breathing "sea air." It was there where I first saw the Chinese *amahs*. The blue-smocked and pants-clad women walked with an unusual gait. They took very tiny steps, walking so unsteadily that they appeared about to topple over as they walked.

I remember asking Isabel, "Why do they walk that way?"

"Because when they were little girls, their feet were bound so that they wouldn't get large."

"Why?" I asked, getting more curious about these women.

"Oh, the Chinese believed that having small feet made the women beautiful."

"Will I ever get my feet bound?"

"No, child. We Filipinos do not do that. I think they have also stopped foot binding in China," she replied.

These Chinese women came to the Philippines to work as children's nursemaids. Their shoes looked as small as mine, and I was about five. The women I saw were about my aunt's age, fifty, with cropped, straight dark hair. While the rest of the maids taking care of children socialized, the *amahs* did not mingle. They spoke rarely, and their Tagalog was broken. Most knew English and were favored by the foreign and well-to-do families, like the von Gieses. Years later, after I saw penguins walk, I remembered the unsteady gait of the Chinese *amahs*.

Mr. von Giese had been employed by the Japanese government as a locksmith specializing in opening safes. The Japanese did not bother them because he was German and worked for them. They lived comfortably during the Japanese occupation. They ate well, and food shortages were unknown in their part of Manila. Had it not been for the presence of a few Japanese sentries at strategic corners of Ermita, they would not have noticed we were at war with the Japanese. The girls continued their schooling at a nearby convent. Life went on as usual for them.

Not long after moving in with us, Mr. von Giese found a job with the American Army opening safes abandoned in bombed-out offices. It did not take long for the American authorities to review his record and clear him. They needed men with special talents like him. The von Giese family found a house some distance from us, thanked us profusely, and left. They soon went back to their former routine. Nena and I were sad to see them go. We had gotten accustomed to playing with the girls.

Sometime later, I overhead my brother Vic asking my father about them.

"Have you heard any news of the von Gieses since they went away, Papá?"

"Indirectly, I heard he was hired by the American Army."

"Why would the Americans hire someone who worked for the Japanese?"

"Well, sometimes the Americans do not look too closely at who they hire as long as the person is needed to do a specific job. There aren't many safe crackers in Manila."

"I was hoping cousin Patricia would at least drop by and say hello or something."

"I wouldn't count on it. We probably won't be hearing from them again."

Some years later, when I was in my teens, I read about the three von Giese girls. They had become champion swimmers, and their pictures appeared in the sports section of the local newspapers frequently. They had grown up to be beautiful young ladies. They were taller, their long hair still blonde, and their thin bodies had become fuller. But we never saw nor heard from them again. They disappeared from our life as suddenly as they came.

CHAPTER 18
Normal Life Resumes

LIFE SLOWLY RETURNED TO "NORMAL" once the war ended in 1945. However, almost everything was different from how it had been before the war. Everyone in Manila was trying to rebuild their families, their homes, and their lives. People needed to recover their health and their habits. Many men needed to find work. Previous activities were resumed, for better or worse.

Slowly, our life improved little by little, in large and small ways. For example, when my father received a very large shipment of yellow and blue cotton fabric, we were finally able to put up curtains on our windows. But we also had to be satisfied with using the same material for our dresses and pillow and bed covers. We shared this yellow and blue calico with some of our cousins. It was very funny to see all of us dressed in this fabric, blending with the pillows, curtains, and bedspreads. Our maids used the same fabric for their aprons.

About a year later, things had improved a lot. Fe celebrated her eighteenth birthday with a big party in one of the downtown hotels. Since Nena and I were still too young, we were not allowed to go. After her birthday party, Fe was featured as a cover girl in one of the Sunday magazines. She looked so pretty on the cover, wearing a black dress with a V-neckline, showing off a strand of pearls, a far cry from the blue and yellow calico.

My teeth were the only casualties of the war for me. During the war, hygiene was not our highest priority. I rarely brushed my teeth, and I ate anything I could get my hands on. During the war, I would frequently wake up in the middle of the night in incredible pain because of a toothache. My father would take me to a dentist when he could, but there was no anesthesia during the war. Dr. Ana, our dentist, would give me a perfume-soaked cotton ball to place on my cavity. Then she would vainly try to fill the tooth with a temporary filling, all she had available. But it would always fall out as soon as I bit into something hard. Luckily, my father insisted that my bad teeth not be pulled out, so fortunately, I still have them today.

Despite Dr. Ana's kindness and sweet smile, I dreaded seeing her. The sound of the foot-driven drill petrified me. The pain it inflicted sent shivers up and down my spine. Even though I hated those trips to the dentist, somehow I never learned to brush my teeth well enough. Years later, I would scold my own daughters to brush their teeth after every meal. I would tell them about my experiences with Dr. Ana and repeat, over and over, "You don't want your teeth to be like mine. No one told me to brush my teeth because I didn't have a mother." It must have worked because my older daughter never had a cavity, and my younger daughter only had a few.

After the war, my father heard of a dentist trained in the United States, and he took us to see Dr. Carpio. We went by bus. It was the first time that we had been downtown since liberation. I was shocked to see so many buildings burned or pockmarked with bullet or shrapnel holes. I could not recognize the street where we used to walk on our way to our first elementary school. Some buildings stood intact next to skeletons of other buildings.

Dr. Carpio's office was in an elegant part of Manila, but, at the time of our dental appointments, few buildings there remained intact. His office was in one of the older high-rise (six-floor) office buildings that had escaped bombing. The lobby was dark, and the elevator barely worked. An old man sat on a stool inside the elevator, ready to take anyone up and down the building. I was scared of the slow, creaking elevator and the wrinkled, old man, and held tightly to my father's hand on every visit.

Dr. Carpio was probably in his forties. He had thinning hair and wore rimless glasses. He and Maria, his competent dental assistant, worked on my teeth over several weeks. She looked crisp in her white uniform. She made sure I was comfortable and didn't suffer much. For the first time in my life, I received anesthesia injected into my gums by a long needle. My only discomfort came from getting the injection and having my mouth wide open for hours at a time. It was quite an ordeal, but I knew my teeth needed fixing. After each dental appointment, my father treated Nena and me to vanilla ice cream in paper cups, bought at a nearby stand, eaten with a wooden spoon like a tongue depressor.

Dr. Carpio efficiently drilled every cavity and then refilled it, no matter its size, with gold. My mouth looked like a mini-gold mine, and when I smiled, I glistened. Even my front teeth were capped with gold. Not until I came to the United States some years later and saw everyone with white teeth, did the golden appearance of my mouth bother me. I had my American dentist replace all the gold fillings and caps with porcelain.

Although our own neighborhood had not suffered the kind of damage to buildings that we saw downtown, the same could not be said for the street. Walking to school along Washington Street was full of adventures. The street was not paved and did not have storm drains except for narrow ditches running alongside it. During rainy season, it was often flooded. I had to wade in knee-deep water and share the road with frogs, floating worms, and other amphibious animals. To prevent getting splashed by passing cars, I opened my umbrella and shielded my body whenever a car passed by. Sometimes, horses pulling *calesas* would miss their footing and fall into the narrow ditches. It would often take a group of men with strong arms to pull out the horse and the carriage. I had to wear wooden shoes, *bakya*, to school since leather shoes did not last long when often submerged in muddy water.

In the summer, there was no standing water. Instead, speeding cars created a storm of dust, contributing to everyone's discomfort. Servants from different houses along Washington Street would often ladle the black water from the storm ditches, which often contained raw sewage, onto the dry street to dampen it and cut down on the dust. I did not know which I preferred: the dust that caused us to sneeze or the smelly sewage on the street. I always used my handkerchief to cover my nose as I walked on Washington Street.

My father's business resumed after the war. The Arlegui house was remodeled and converted fully to commercial use. A small private college and a lawyer occupied the upstairs where we used to live. My father's sales office for photostats, blue and white printing, supplies for schools, artists, engineers, and architects took over the downstairs. The business had started to prosper, so my father no longer worked as a surveyor. Instead, he focused full time on his business.

My father employed some of his relatives, including my *Tío* Delfin and one of my cousins, the oldest son of *Tía* Josefa and *Tío* Enrique, who was a lawyer. He worked for my father as his manager and personal representative. Since my father did not speak English, my cousin acted on his behalf when it came time to negotiate and write contracts.

However, a rift developed between my father and this cousin so that all business and personal connections between them were severed. After the break-up, my cousin went on to start a competing business against my father.

"There's enough work for both of us," my father said. The war ending had created lots of orders for photostatic and blueprint work. My cousin followed my father's business model, down to the Vespas used by the delivery boys. Whenever I would ask my father what caused the rift, my father would say, "He's a lawyer, I don't want to be sued."

Tío Delfin worked at my father's import-export business opening doors every morning and locking up in the evening. In his fifties, married with six children, he was my father's youngest brother. Everyone at work liked him. He often substituted for the cashier when the latter was out.

I often wondered why he was not an engineer like my other uncle, *Tío* Mianong, a successful civil engineer with a degree from the University of Illinois in Urbana-Champaign (my father had paid for his education). It turned out that my father did send *Tío* Delfin to the university to study, but he preferred cock fighting to studying. He spent a great deal of his time studying gaming cocks, and pruning and combing his fighting roosters. Cock fighting, which had been illegal before the war, was now tolerated. It was common to see cockfights in someone's backyard, feathers and dust flying in the air, and hear the struggling noise from the fighting cocks, the loud cheers from the winners, and the groans and moans from the losers. Money changed hands among friends and neighbors as quickly as the fighting roosters routed each other.

Every Sunday morning, men left their wives and children, skipped church, and took their sons, roosters, and money to a small cockfight arena in La Loma, north of our house just on the outskirts of Manila. Among the hundreds of men that passed by our house would be my *Tío* Delfin, dressed in a white shirt, khaki pants, wearing a Panama hat and shiny black shoes, holding his white rooster with the red crown on the crook of his left arm. He would be followed by my 14-year-old cousin, Benny, carrying an empty rattan cage.

Later that day at dusk, after the fights, we would see a stream of losers walking slowly home, including *Tío* Delfin, with heads bowed, shoulders stooped, solemn faces, dead roosters held upside down by their legs, lost in thought, as if thinking of what might have been. The sons, including my cousin Benny, followed them, walking jauntily, thinking perhaps of chicken soup and *tinola*, a chicken dish with squash.

There were other strains within my family during this period. One especially painful one occurred between my father and my Tío Mianong. This uncle, who was a major in the Philippine Army, was captured early in the war. He spent the war years as a prisoner of the Japanese. He asked my father to look after his family. My father did his best to make sure his brother's family had a roof over their heads and food to eat.

His daughter Estrella was the apple of my *Tío* Mianong's eye. She was his only daughter, the oldest of four children. Her fair smooth skin, long dark hair in a single braid, and evenly spaced dark brown eyes, high cheeks and slender nose complemented her alert expression and keen mind. She was always at the top of her class in school, and my uncle had visions of her being a doctor or lawyer.

Across from their house, a small guard house was built by the authorities on the rotunda, from which policemen guarded the intersection of Dimasalang and Washington streets. Two young policemen each took turns staying in the small guardhouse. There was very little traffic since, due to lack of gasoline, all cars had been abandoned, leaving only horse-drawn *calesas* and *carretelas*. The two policemen became acquainted with my aunt Ising and her children, and the younger one, Oscar, became a frequent visitor to my uncle's house. Rumors started to fly that there was something going on between my aunt and the young Oscar, but everyone was wrong. Before anyone suspected their plans, Estrella married Oscar. My uncle was furious when he returned home from prison to find out that Estrella was married to a policeman and was pregnant with his child. She had abandoned plans to go to the University. She had lost her youthful looks, gotten fat, and cut her beautiful long black hair short. Instead of getting angry with his wife and daughter for her imprudent marriage, my uncle blamed my father for permitting the marriage. Although the two brothers still spoke to one another, things were never the same.

In the period immediately following the war, people began to become reacquainted with their neighbors. I came to know Pilar, who was two years older than I was, the same age as Nena. She lived with her family in a small wooden unpainted chalet with a thatched roof at the approach to Vision Street. She became one of our regular playmates even though she attended a different school. Pilar was tall for her age, very much like her father, a very large man who worked as a government clerk. I didn't see much of him, but he frightened me because of his menacing appearance.

Pilar had short curly black hair, small dark lips and eyes, and long legs. She talked so softly that you could barely hear her. Her mother talked even more quietly. But I liked both mother and daughter because they were quiet, kind, and unassuming.

Unlike the other mothers in the neighborhood who quarreled and spent their time gossiping, Mrs. Silvestre was short and thin with short curly hair. She mainly kept to herself and was barely seen outside her home. I occasionally saw her hanging the family laundry in their backyard. She always gave me a smile of recognition whenever I passed by.

Every afternoon after school, Pilar would come to our house to play. But every day at exactly five o'clock, even if we were in the middle of an exciting game, her brother, Tony, would come and shout through the door.

"Pilar, Mamá needs you to go to the market!"

"I'm coming." Pilar would shout back, and before we could say anything, she would be out of our house.

How we hated those interruptions.

One day, my sister Nena, and I decided to accompany Pilar to the Blumentritt open market to find out what was so important for her to buy every day in the middle of our play. Because we did not have bus fare, we walked for more than ten blocks to the market. Although it was late in the afternoon, the market was still teeming with shoppers haggling and merchants shouting to passersby to buy their goods.

I couldn't keep my eyes off the beautifully arranged oranges and grapes on boxes marked "Produce of the U.S.A," raw white rice heaped high on round rattan baskets, and slaughtered chickens with feathers still on, throats slit, hanging from hooks. The smell of rotting fish competed with the aroma of ripened mangoes. Pilar tugged at my arm. "Katinka, we better hurry before the store closes."

Pilar maneuvered us through different food stalls until we reached one that sold mostly beverages. I was thirsty and wanted a Coke. But we didn't have any money with us. The woman was expecting her. She handed Pilar a package, wrapped in brown paper, and we walked back home in silence.

"What's in the package, Pilar?" I finally asked.

Pilar was too embarrassed to respond.

"Can we peek inside? Promise, we won't tell."

"Here. It's just a bottle of rum for my father," Pilar admitted sheepishly as she opened the package.

It seemed that Mr. Silvestre enjoyed a bottle of rum every day after work but did not want to be seen buying it. He sent Pilar instead to get it for him. Although Pilar never talked about it, there were rumors in the neighborhood that her father beat her mother when he was drunk at night.

CHAPTER 19

The Governess

AFTER THE WAR, MY FATHER TOOK A GOOD LOOK at his five motherless children and felt that the younger ones needed guidance and perhaps some lessons on manners. During the war, the question of survival was more important than manners and disciplining children. My father was more concerned about our safety and whether we had food to eat. We occasionally got spanked with a belt or slippers for misbehaving, but we were more often allowed to get away with behavior not tolerated during peacetime.

I was the youngest, nine years old, and I must admit I was on the wild side. I did not listen to anyone, did not follow a bedtime, played and stayed out of doors till exhaustion forced me in, talked in a loud voice, quarreled with my siblings, and had atrocious table manners. No one took responsibility for our clothes, so often I wore torn clothes to school. Bathing depended on whim. I rarely brushed my teeth.

My father decided to hire a governess to teach us manners and good behavior. Miss Sison came from a formerly wealthy family that lost its fortune during the war. She was highly recommended as a governess by some friends of my father. The war was cruel to families, like the Sisons, who sold off properties during the war, thinking that afterwards the sale would be invalidated. These families tried to get their properties back by means of lawsuits, but the judgment went against them. Others frittered away their savings and earnings during the Japanese occupation, thinking it was only "funny" money. We knew of several families where the father stopped working and earning income, having assumed the war would not last long.

Miss Sison was about forty when she came to work as our governess. She was tall, very light in complexion, with black hair parted in the middle and tied in a bun. She stared at you like a hawk. Her smile was as rare as a blue diamond. She wore white, looked like a nurse, but did not smell like one. She towered over us and, had she tried, could have lifted any one of us children without much effort. Her sour expression and booming voice inspired fear and attention. I could hear her calling me from three houses away. I thought Miss Sison was in the wrong occupation. She repelled children. I must say something good about her: she taught us how to speak English, and she did not lay a hand on us.

Schools had just reopened, and English was the medium of instruction. My father feared that we would be behind in school. Even though I was nine years old, I was just starting second grade again. Earlier, my father had employed a neighbor, Mrs. Guerrero, an English teacher at a high school, to be our English tutor after school. She lived next door and came to our house to help with homework and give instructions on English grammar and speech. But an incident with her fruit salad ended the arrangement.

Mrs. Guerrero did not own a refrigerator and used to put some of her food in our refrigerator. One day, she was giving a party and asked if she could put her large bowl of fruit salad in our refrigerator. My brother Paking, who always had a large appetite, did not know of the arrangement and had assumed what was in the refrigerator was ours to eat. So in a fit of hunger, he ate all of Mrs. Guerrero's fruit salad. We were very embarrassed to discover Paking had eaten her salad by mistake. Mrs. Guerrero was deeply annoyed to find she had no food to serve her guests. Despite apologies and replacement of her salad a day later, our relationship with Mrs. Guerrero became strained, and the English lessons stopped.

That's when Miss Sison came into our lives. She did not actually live with us because we had no room for her. She arrived punctually at six o'clock in the morning by bus, dressed from head to toe in white, woke us up, helped Nena and me get dressed for school, and ate with us. As a result, I finally learned to brush my teeth regularly. She made sure we used forks and knives instead of our hands and that we cut our food with a knife instead of a spoon. She helped with homework, tutored us in English grammar and spelling, darned our old clothes and bought new ones, supervised the preparation and serving of meals, and made sure we followed a regular bedtime.

She replaced chaos with order in our house and lives. Maids used to peel my shrimps, remove bones from my fish and chicken, and do almost everything except spoon-feed me. The maid also shampooed my hair, braided it every morning, helped me dress, and tied my shoes. I was nine and still dependent on a maid to help me get dressed for school. Miss Sison put a stop to that. I learned to do many things a girl my age needed to do on her own.

My table manners, appearance, and demeanor also improved. My father beamed with pride at the dining table. He no longer had to remind us to cut our meat with a knife. I learned to be courteous and polite.

I arrived in school wearing clean, mended, and color-coordinated clothes. I had also bathed and had the fresh smell of Palmolive soap. My hair, recently shampooed, was in two braids and free of lice. I started getting good grades in Health and Appearance in school. Before the start of classes, all the students had to lay their hands on top of their desks, palms down, to show clean and clipped fingernails. If I had dirty hands or fingernails, the teacher would slap them with a long stick that she carried around with her and give me a failing grade for that day. Every morning in school, I had to show the teacher that I had brought a clean handkerchief pinned to my dress. I received a failing grade for the day without that handkerchief. This is one habit I still have. I cannot leave the house without carrying a clean handkerchief.

I wish I could say that we grew to love Miss Sison for all she did for us. Even though I started receiving compliments on my appearance, I never felt comfortable with Miss Sison. She was very hard to please. The war years had spoiled us. We had been given too much freedom. It was difficult to have to answer to an adult other than my father. We just could not live under her rules. Sometimes, her critical comments about my manners or clothing made me cry. Soon, a conflict arose between my brothers and Miss Sison.

"Why do we have to have a governess?" complained twelve-year-old Vic to my father.

"She is controlling who I can play with. We are grown boys. Why do we have to go to bed early?" asked Paking.

My father looked at the boys and thought for a while. "Well, perhaps we can compromise," he said. "How about having Miss Sison take care of just Nena and Katinka. You don't have to answer to her. But that does not mean you can do whatever you want. Is that understood?"

That seemed to have satisfied the boys. Their complaints decreased. But soon, another conflict emerged at the dining table.

Miss Sison was talking to my father in private, one day, after dinner.

"Mr. Floro," she said. "Does Macario have to eat with us? Shouldn't he be eating with the other servants since he's the family chauffeur?"

My father got red in the face. He had always treated Macario as one of the family. Macario had been driving for us since before the war. My father trusted him implicitly. In fact, we were allowed to go anywhere as long as Macario drove us to our destination and waited for us. When my father eventually bought a car for his personal use, a 1948 white Dodge sedan, he hired his company's chauffeur, Macario, to be our personal driver.

Macario was the opposite of Tino, *Inay's* driver. Tino was a good-looking young man who loved to flirt with the young servants in the house. He used lots of pomade to sleek back his long black wavy hair, and I smelled cologne on him. Three housemaids ended up having his children, and they had to leave. My father insisted that Tino not drive his daughters around town alone. I don't know why *Inay* kept him on since she was such a strict Catholic, but since he also acted as a bodyguard for *Inay's* son, Corong, the latter must have convinced his mother of Tino's importance.

Whereas Tino was young, handsome, and a womanizer, Macario was short, dark, and a solid family man. He could be trusted with young girls. My father admired his steadfastness and patience with children.

Macario's driving record was impeccable except for one occasion when he was jailed for speeding. Anyone who knew Macario's cautious driving habits couldn't believe it when a policeman ticketed him for speeding and jailed him. He must not have flashed the usual five pesos all drivers inserted with their driver's license when he was stopped by that policeman. My father had to go to the police station to pay his fine before they would release him.

"Miss Sison, I appreciate what you have done for this family, especially with my young daughters. You have turned them into well-mannered young ladies, and I am grateful. However, you must understand that Macario is considered part of this family. He has been a faithful employee for a great number of years. I value his loyalty and service. And I trust him. He shall continue eating with us. I am sorry if this bothers you. You are free to consider another position."

Miss Sison was surprised at my father's reply. She thought that her work with us had been very successful and much appreciated, which it was. She assumed my father would side with her over the Macario issue. Miss Sison came from an old aristocratic family where servants wore uniforms, bowed before their masters, ate different food, and were treated as if they were inferior to the family. It was the opposite at our house. Miss Sison did not count on my father's respect for Macario.

"Very well, sir, I shall be leaving your house next week. I just cannot accept having my meals with a chauffeur."

True to her word, Miss Sison left us. I don't remember crying when she gave notice, even though I did appreciate what she did for us. Let's just say there was more joy than sadness at her departure, especially from the boys. She was cold and unfeeling, not an affectionate person. Also, I think Miss Sison had aspirations of becoming Mrs. Floro, which no one else wanted, especially my father. I was happy not to be getting a stepmother.

CHAPTER 20

Albert Elementary School

AS SOON AS PEACE WAS ESTABLISHED throughout the islands in 1945, it was decreed that schools would reopen after teachers were hired. Thus, I found myself on a Monday morning, together with my siblings and hundreds of children, in front of Dr. Alejandro Albert Elementary School, where flowers bloomed in a garden normally off limits to children. We all sang the national anthems of the Philippines and the USA and pledged allegiance to two flags as they were raised up the flagpole. This practice continued until our independence on July 4, 1946.

Many parents had withheld their children from attending school during the Japanese occupation. For many, this school was their first in over three years. The students varied in ages and height for each grade. I was the second shortest pupil in second grade even though I was already nine years old. Every morning, we lined up from shortest to tallest, girls and boys in separate rows, before entering our classroom.

Inside, we sat two students to a desk meant for one pupil. Each teacher taught more than sixty students. The blackboards covered the top half of the front wall of the schoolroom. We had very few textbooks. Everything was either dictated by the teacher or written on the blackboard. We had to go to the blackboard to solve arithmetic problems or spell out words. Since I had been doing this at home, arithmetic presented very little problem for me, unlike many of my classmates, who were seeing these types of problems for the first time.

Paper and pencils were in short supply, so a whole sheet of paper was torn into halves, then into fourths, to use during exams, which were dictated by teachers. We were not allowed to waste paper. Every scrap was used. Fortunately, I had an advantage over my classmates. My father's office had started selling school supplies and textbooks, so that I had an abundant supply of paper, pencils, fountain pens, and notebooks. I was the only one in my class to have a Parker 21 pen engraved with my name in gold lettering (my father's business also did engraving).

Textbooks, supplied by the schools in the early grades, were shared, two students per book. They were passed out to the class by monitors at the beginning of class and collected at the end of the session. Some textbooks had to be purchased by the students. Since the schools provided no lockers, students had to carry their own books to school every day. I carried the heaviest load of textbooks as I got into the fourth and upper grades. Walking and carrying a heavy load for more than a mile to school, in the rain or heat, kept me lean and fit. But I still see today the marks imprinted on my left arm that my book bag left.

The janitor, *Mang* Juan, a dark, stocky man with a scarred face, terrified me. He exercised dictatorial powers the same as the principal. We had to remove and carry our shoes or *bakya* before entering the hallways in order to keep them clean. The janitor's authority extended to the outside grounds. As part of our curriculum, in Gardening class, we were assigned plots of land to plant vegetable seeds and cultivate them. I planted corn that grew taller than I was and beans that climbed out of their stakes. But watering and taking care of them almost resulted in my being expelled from school. The janitor enforced a rule that forbade watering plants outside of class hours because of frequent vandalism by other students. If he caught someone in the garden outside of class hours, he reported the student to the principal, and expulsion was a likely result.

One day during the dry season, my friend, Rosalie, and I noticed that our corn was dying from lack of water. Our concern for our dying corn, its stalk yellow and brittle, overcame our fear of the janitor. We watered our plants after school was let out. We were as short as the growing corn stalks, which hid us from the prying eyes of the janitor. But not for long. We soon realized our mistake when we heard the voice of the janitor, as if using a microphone, threatening us. We hid behind the corn stalks and beans as he pursued us like criminals. We were lucky that he did not catch us nor recognize who we were.

Rosalie and I, who were normally talkative, did not breathe a word of our adventure to anyone, especially to our teacher, Miss Bautista. We were just happy not to have been caught. We did learn our lesson and never watered our plants again outside of school hours. Our corn did grow and survive, and we harvested the sweet ears to be cooked during Home Economics and sold during our school lunch hour.

In addition to *Mang* Juan's responsibility as an enforcer, he also cleaned the hallways, bathrooms, and the principal's office, but not the classrooms. It was the school monitors who kept the classrooms clean every day after class. As a member of an elite group of volunteer monitors, I often stayed late after school in order to erase the blackboards, sweep, and polish the floor. In my own home, I never laid a hand on a broom or a mop. But in school, I vied with other students to be given the opportunity to sweep the floor and take part in the weekly waxing and polishing. The waxing was hard work. We had to apply paste wax weekly by hand, on our hands and knees. Polishing and buffing was more fun as each child sat on a large piece of rag to be pulled by another all over the room, polishing the floor at the same time. To maintain the children's enthusiasm for cleanliness, prizes were given by the principal for the cleanest room every month. We took great pride in our clean homerooms.

Our teacher taught us to stand and greet every visitor who came to our classroom. The principal used to come and visit our classroom often, more often than any other classroom. Since we had to remain quiet while he was in the room, we reacted to each of his visits by rolling our eyes and smiling at one another, as if we were in on a secret. We all thought the principal was sweet on our teacher.

Miss Elenita Bautista, in her early twenties, with shoulder-length brown hair, clear complexion, and almond-shaped brown eyes, was probably the prettiest teacher in the whole school. Legs badly scarred would have detracted from her appearance had she not worn hard-to-get opaque silk stockings to cover them. I, too, developed a skin infection during the war that led to scarring. Malnutrition was the culprit.

Corporal punishment by teachers and principal was the rule. I never saw the principal punish a student since this was done behind the closed doors of his office. But teachers routinely held long sticks for pointing at the words on the blackboard or hitting children's hands or head. A typical teacher's response to a misbehaving child was to pull his ear and twist it. Parents expected their children to be disciplined by the teachers using corporal punishment since they themselves did the same things to recalcitrant sons and daughters.

Miss Bautista disciplined our class not by hitting us, but by kind words and gentle admonitions. She had a very sweet, musical voice. Just one look from her quieted the noisiest student. She made learning fun. We all vied for her attention. I was thrilled to be one of her favorites.

One day while I was walking to school, a big truck sprayed water on me as it sped by, soaking me completely from head to toes. Since I was near the school, I decided to continue. My wet hair and dripping dress caused a sensation among my classmates, and I saw a look of anguish on Miss Bautista's face. She decided to take me home so that I could change into dry clothes. She left the class under the care of another teacher and stopped a passing two-ton truck, much to the surprise of its driver, to take us to my home. There were no telephones then to call my father or my governess. I arrived home in the middle of the school day, dripping wet, accompanied by my second-grade teacher. I had never seen Miss Sison so surprised.

What Miss Bautista did for me was extremely unusual, as unusual then as it would be today in the United States. Teachers simply did not leave their classes, no matter what the needs of their students were. I never saw another teacher making a compassionate act towards a student; they were just too overworked. Even if they started out as compassionate people, during those years right after the war, they often became mainly disciplinarians in order to handle classes of sixty or more children, all at different levels. My father sent a basket of *lanzones*, grape-sized yellow-skinned fruit in clusters, to Miss Bautista in appreciation.

One day, as we were nearing the end of the school year, Miss Bautista lined up her second grade students, from the shortest to the tallest. We varied in ages from six to twelve. I was nine going on ten. Together with the other children who could already read and write, I was taken to another classroom where we were asked to read from a book and to divide and multiply a series of numbers. Those who could read and solve the arithmetic problems correctly were skipped to fourth grade (the others were skipped one grade, to third grade). When I was later promoted to sixth grade, bypassing fifth, I was sorry to have missed being taught how to tat, to make lace, in fifth grade.

I owed my arithmetic skills to my father, a surveyor, who always tutored and drilled us in arithmetic. During the war years, while we were in and out of school, he always made a point of teaching us addition, subtraction, division, and multiplication in Spanish. I learned mostly by watching my brothers and sisters as they worked on the blackboard. One of the exercises I remember was his writing a long series of numbers in a column to be added correctly in the shortest time possible. The fastest and most accurate won a commendation. Cousins who came to our house were challenged in arithmetic. My father was so proud of me when I beat an older cousin, who cried at his defeat.

I felt sad to leave the kind and beautiful Miss Bautista. My new fourth grade teacher, Mr. de los Santos, turned out to be a man with a temper. He had lost his right arm during the war and wore his right sleeve dangling from his shoulder. He was short, bald, and always wore a blue long-sleeved shirt. His fourth grade class, section B-6, was a combination of the newly promoted second graders and the most unruly children in the fourth grade.

Mr. de los Santos controlled the class by throwing an eraser with his left arm at the misbehaving student. Sometimes, if he heard someone talking while he was writing on the blackboard, he would throw the eraser without turning around and hit the offender.

He showed no mercy towards the boys who were often boisterous and rowdy. But he was kind to the girls, especially the bright ones. I was lucky to have been one of his favorites.

From second grade onward, because I was a good student and never talked out of turn in class, I often became the teacher's favorite. It also helped that my other brothers and sisters ahead of me were excellent students and paved the way for me. Whenever I had a teacher who had taught my older siblings, I didn't have to do anything special for the teacher to favor me. I had an easy life. All I had to do was study and perform according to my abilities. I rarely spoke in class and seldom raised my hand to volunteer answers to questions asked by the teacher. But if called upon, I usually gave the correct answers. I had a fear of speaking in front of the class. Once, in our Music class, I decided that a failing grade was preferable to singing solo in front of the class as everyone had done before me. My Music teacher finally relented and gave me a passing grade based on test results, rather than a song sung in front of the class.

Although we were not taught instrumental music in grade school, we did a lot of singing and dancing. School children were taught folk dances early on. Every year, I learned a different dance during our physical education classes. At the end of the school year, our school would put on a festival where all the students, in native costumes, staged folk dances. I remember performing once in the company of thousands of elementary school children in the national stadium with the President of the Philippines and other high dignitaries in attendance.

In elementary school, we were taught many skills in Home Economics, among them embroidery, sewing, and cooking. For a sewing class in sixth grade, I had to draft and cut my own pattern and then had to complete a dress for a sewing project that was to be displayed in the school for visitors to see. Even though I had learned how to sew on my mother's Singer treadle sewing machine, courtesy of *Tía* Sisang, I just could not sew straight seams for such an important project. I asked help from our dressmaker. On the day of the exhibit, based on the straight seams and professional finishes of the dresses on display, it appeared as if we were all professional seamstresses. But no one said a word about who had actually sewed the garments.

Somehow, it was not frowned upon if you had someone do your homework or finish your project. I often asked my brother Eddy, who drew very well, to illustrate my projects. Eddy drew all the artwork for me for a project on Longfellow's *Hiawatha,* while I retold the story. As art was not taught in public schools, Eddy had never taken an art class in his life, yet his drawing showed professionalism and great talent. When Pepsi Cola wanted to enter the Philippine market, it held a contest for artists to draw cartoons depicting Pepsi. Eddy's entry showed an East Indian man who played his flute to make his coiled cobra come to life. In his drawing, Eddy substituted Pepsi Cola for the cobra, rising from the coiled position. The caption read, "It's a Pepsi!" He won ten pesos for first prize.

There was an incident in school that has remained with me all these years. A fourth grader, Alma, whom I knew by sight, died in the school playground during recess when she failed to jump over a waist-high rope held taut by two girls. It was a typical game we played during recess. Two girls held a rope or a stick starting from ankle-height. Children jumped over the rope; those who made it continued on to the next round, where the rope was raised a little higher. As the rope reached waist high, fewer girls could accomplish the jump. The trick was to jump over a hurdle as high as one could. Alma was a very good jumper. However, on that day, somehow her foot caught on the rope as she attempted her jump, and she fell headfirst onto the pavement. She died that same day in the hospital. The next day, we gathered in front of the school, amid blooming flowers, a single Filipino flag flying high since we had gained our independence, and with tears in our eyes, sang, "Nearer My God to Thee." I always associate that song with the events of that day in 1947.

After the incident, we were forbidden to play that particular game. Teachers went on patrol to monitor our play. We were limited to skipping rope, playing with balls, and a local game called *sipa* that involves kicking a paper object into the air with your foot as many times as possible.

CHAPTER 21
Calliope Claustro

I WAS CHOSEN TO BE THE SCHOOL VALEDICTORIAN after sixth grade (despite skipping third and fifth grade). I was on cloud nine. It was a foregone conclusion that someone else would write my valedictory speech. I did not understand why the speech had to be in English, since most of us could barely speak it. The only person in our family who spoke and knew English well was my cousin, Eulalio, a lawyer and the manager of my father's firm. I practiced and memorized my ghostwritten speech. I don't remember what it said, and I don't think anybody else cared.

It was the first time in my life that I ever appeared in front of a large audience and gave a speech. I trembled as I stood on the temporary stage in front of about two hundred classmates, teachers, and parents. My voice quivered, and my unsteady hands almost dropped the paper my speech was typed on. My sister told me later I sounded as if I was about to cry.

I received a gold medal, hung from a red, white, and blue ribbon, from our congressman (for the second district). He made sure his name, engraved in big letters on the medal, would remain known to posterity. There was no mention of the recipient or the reason for the medal.

Calliope Claustro came into my life at this time. I thought she was the most beautiful girl at the Dr. A. Albert Elementary School. She was tall for her age and came to school every day with her light brown hair set in curls à la Shirley Temple, the envy of all the girls. She had brown eyes framed by curly brown lashes, oval face, a delicate thin nose, and thick, dark brown lips. She was very fair even though her family came from the Ilocos Norte region, where people tend to be very dark. She stood and walked with very erect posture, a sign of early ballet training.

Before this time, she never talked to me. She did not join any group during recess. I noticed that when called upon by the teacher, she sometimes did not know the correct answers. She spoke in a hush. After the announcement that I was to be the school valedictorian, I received an invitation from Mrs. Claustro to go home with Calliope after school. I had seen Mrs. Claustro wait for Calliope after school in their black T-Ford, the uniformed chauffeur seated in front and Mrs. Claustro seated at the back with the car door open to let in the breeze. I had never realized Mrs. Claustro was even aware of my existence. Since I had envied Calliope's beauty for so long, I was very excited to visit her and did not leave my father alone until he gave permission for me to go.

That afternoon, Mrs. Claustro was wearing a long black dress with matching black shoes and black patent purse, seated on the black leather of a black 1938 T-Ford. The chauffeur wore a black cap, black uniform, and polished black shoes. His black-gloved hands held the black steering wheel of the car. It was the color of mourning. It turned out that Mrs. Claustro was a widow. She stood erect like her daughter, and she was tall and slim. She might have been as good looking as her daughter years ago, but now her hair had turned completely white, and wrinkles had replaced the smooth skin. She looked old enough to be Calliope's grandmother. Calliope was her only child. I noticed from whom Calliope got her thick, dark brown lips.

Calliope and her mother lived in a large old wooden house with a corrugated zinc roof painted pink, in a middle-class area of Manila near the school. Upon entering the fenced front yard, I smelled jasmine and saw the vine reaching up to the sky. Tall mango and acacia trees shaded the house. Pink and magenta bougainvillea ran wild around the iron fence. A low cement ledge by the front held different sizes of terra cotta pots, each one containing various blooming flower plants and other tropical plants with multicolored leaves. I realized Mrs. Calliope loved flowers and had a good gardener. A hose that had recently been used to water the plants lay coiled, resembling a green boa ready to strike at an intruder.

When I entered their living room, I felt transported to another era, one I had only seen in pictures. The decor looked old and foreign to me. The furniture was all upholstered in faded pastel brocade, an unusual sight, since the heat and humidity in Manila made this type of furniture very uncomfortable. The living room walls, painted light green, had a pair of old dark green velvet drapes trimmed with lace, preventing the light from coming in from the outside. All the houses in Manila I knew were built with windows that had translucent square panels of shells that provided light even when they were closed. I had never lived in a house with draperies.

A large ebony grand piano stood at the corner by a large window, open as if ready for a concert. Calliope told me her mother played the piano but that she preferred ballet and dancing. A floral, fringed silk scarf covered part of the piano, adorned with family photographs in silver and wooden frames. Calliope noticed my interest in the photographs and gave me the names of all the subjects. Her father, who had died during the war, appeared in several of the pictures. I could see that Calliope inherited his Caucasian looks. In those years, Filipinos had absorbed the Caucasian standard of beauty; I had been told all my life that a fair complexion was beautiful.

A uniformed young maid served us *merienda* consisting of various kinds of cake and Coca-Cola in the large dining room. We ate on a massive round oak table with curved feet. A handsome buffet with mirrors, decorated with elaborate hand carving, Filipino-style, stood opposite the dining table. The dining room, in contrast to the living room, was uncurtained and very airy. The high ceiling was painted blue like the sky. French doors opened to an outside garden facing the back yard. Again, I was greeted by blooming potted plants and flowers and flowering bushes. The backyard reminded me of a botanical garden we used to visit before war broke out.

Mrs. Claustro was friendly, courteous, and solicitous during our *merienda,* but I felt intimidated by the questions she asked while we were eating. She wanted to know where I lived, how many siblings were in my family, what my father did for a living, and so on. Never in my whole life had I thanked my father for having hired a governess to teach us table manners, but, on this occasion, I silently gave thanks to him. I would have been too embarrassed had I not known how to use a spoon and fork properly. At that stage in my life, I had never been in a stranger's house, let alone someone who was rich and formal. Most of our relatives and friends had modest homes and ate informally, sometimes with their hands.

Afterwards, she left Calliope and me to play alone. Calliope showed me her collection of dolls. It filled a whole armoire. I was ashamed to tell Calliope I had only one doll, which I had received as a gift for Christmas.

Mrs. Claustro must have approved of me because Calliope and I started playing together regularly during recess. We did not sit near each other in class, so that we did not have a chance to talk much. Our classroom was large, consisting of more than sixty boisterous students. Our teacher, Mrs. Perez, had the habit of pairing a noisy boy with a quiet girl, so Calliope and I sat at opposite corners of the room, sharing old scratched-up desks with two hyperactive boys. I often stayed after school to volunteer as a monitor because I enjoyed cleaning and waxing the floor, something I was not allowed to do at home. But Calliope's mother did not wish for her to be a monitor, so she went directly home after school.

I became a regular visitor to their home after my first visit. The invitation was issued a day ahead so that I could get permission from my father. But I never invited Calliope to our house because I was ashamed of it. It was overcrowded, and the neighborhood was not "nice." Calliope never said a word about not seeing where I lived.

On graduation day, Mrs. Claustro brought her own photographer to school and made sure he took a picture of Calliope and me together. Much later, when I was 18 and preparing for my trip to the United States, I came upon that old photograph, taken when I was 12. I was holding hands with Calliope, each one of us smiling self-consciously at the photographer, who probably had just teased us enough to elicit the right kind of smile from his subjects. Even though the photograph was in sepia, I still remember what we wore: a white eyelet cotton dress with a blue taffeta sash around the waist and a wide round collar.

My black patent shoes and white socks contrasted with Calliope's pink socks and white shoes. She looked radiant with a pink ribbon tied around her curly light brown hair. Her antique lace dress had a round neckline intertwined with narrow pink silk satin ribbons.

There was a small reception inside the building where we drank some lemonade and ate little squares of native cakes. Then Mrs. Claustro, accompanied by a man with a large tripod and camera, took Calliope and me to the front of the school—a spot where flowers tended by the janitor bloomed constantly and where children were forbidden to go—to pose for a picture. I used to look at that photograph of Calliope and me, which I have since lost, and wonder what had happened to her. I missed her quiet demeanor and beauty. She went to a Catholic high school while I attended the University of the Philippines High School, where Paking and Nena were enrolled. Calliope's mother never invited me to her house again after that day.

CHAPTER 22

Aling Fidela, My Stepmother

ALING FIDELA HAD WORKED FOR MY FATHER DURING THE WAR selling jewelry. She was in her early forties, supporting a consumptive husband and five children. Her complexion was very light for a Filipina. Long bobby pins held back her brown, frizzy, shoulder-length hair, which she pulled back and knotted into a bun. Her round face, appearing almost flat, was devoid of make-up except for a hint of color on the lips. Her dresses were simply cut and made of ordinary cotton. One noticed her shapely legs marred by shin splints.

After the war, the first time I saw *Aling* Fidela again was after one of our dental appointments in Escolta. My father took us to visit *Aling* Fidela and her family. Her husband had since died. She now ran a food stall in the Quiapo market where she and a niece sold *pancit luglog,* a rice noodle dish with a fish sauce, as popular in the Philippines as spaghetti with meat sauce is in the United States. She told us she had a reputation for selling the best *pancit luglog* in the whole area. She also sold *halo-halo,* an ice-cold dessert made of fruits poached in syrup and topped with crushed ice or ice cream. People from all over Manila came to her food stall to eat.

Her house was a block away from the busy and noisy market. Local Chinese merchants had rebuilt the badly-damaged street with a row of wooden, two-story houses all sharing common walls. The unpainted, narrow houses had no windows facing the street. The only opening to the street in *Aling* Fidela's house was the main door, three-fourths the size of a normal door. I had to bend my head and at the same time lift my feet over the high threshold in order to enter the house. The living room was lit by a bare bulb suspended from the ceiling. A small courtyard at the back gave daylight to the kitchen and small dining room. Clothes hung on clotheslines in the courtyard, which was all concrete with no green plants or shrubs.

We had dinner with *Aling* Fidela and her children. I thought it was the best meal I had had in a long time. She prepared *pancit luglog* and *adobo*. I was then eleven years old. Her youngest daughter was two years older than me, and the two older daughters were already in high school. There were also two sons, the oldest, eighteen, and the youngest, seven. I do not remember much about our first meeting with her children, because we were all too shy to speak to one another.

We were invited to eat with them many more times. One day, just before entering their house, I asked my father why we were going to *Aling* Fidela's house so often. My father paused, looked at Nena and me, and said, "So that you'll have a mother."

Nena and I were shocked to hear this. We all had lived together for the last few years without benefit of a mother, after leaving *Tía* Emilia's house, and I thought we didn't need anyone else (this was after Miss Sison had left).

Many of my relatives, mostly aunts and older women cousins, did not like the idea of my father remarrying. They thought *Aling* Fidela was too old (she was 42), had too many children (five), was too poor, and not very pretty. But her age and lack of beauty commended her to other relatives, who said that at least she could never bear children and thus couldn't place a claim on my father's money. They were almost right; *Aling* Fidela did conceive a child with my father, but she miscarried and had to have a hysterectomy. Her lack of beauty was considered a virtue, for it would make her faithful.

My *Tía* Emilia also objected to our spending time with *Aling* Fidela's daughters. She said that the two older daughters had a bad reputation; they had "easy virtue." At the time, I did not understand what my aunt meant. One evening before my father and *Aling* Fidela got married, the two families, ours and hers, went to the movies together. I sat next to Rita, the oldest daughter who was then seventeen. She, in turn, sat next to my brother Paking, who was fourteen. As soon as the theater got dark, I sensed some motion from where Rita sat. I looked in her direction and saw her kissing and necking with Paking. I was so shocked, but I never breathed a word of this to anyone, not even to Nena.

Forty years later, I mentioned this to Paking, and he laughed. He admitted he and Rita were kissing that night. Had she known, I am sure that my *Tía* Emilia would have been outraged. In those days, a girl's reputation was highly prized, and she undoubtedly thought a close association with *Aling* Fidela's daughters would "tarnish our reputation."

A few months later, my father and *Aling* Fidela got married and went on their honeymoon to Hong Kong and Bangkok by ship. The problem of how to mesh two large families (my father at the time had all of his seven children living with him) was solved by my father purchasing an apartment building on Gunao Street, almost next door to the Arlegui house, for *Aling* Fidela and her children. *Aling* Fidela spent her evenings and nights with my father and his children at Vision Street. During the day, she drove with him to attend to her food business in the Quiapo market and spent some time with her children. She hired servants to take care of her children.

Our two families, my father's and *Aling* Fidela's, eventually got along well. Since we did not live in the same house, seeing each other only in the evenings or on weekends, very little friction arose out of our blended but separate families. By this time, only Nena and I remained at the house on Vision Street (our older siblings were away at college). We had two servants to attend to us. The cook was dismissed, and our food came mostly as take-outs from Chinese restaurants. I loved Cantonese food. Every night I enjoyed Chinese meals from the best restaurants in Manila.

My stepmother became our companion. She accompanied Nena and me to the movies, to the dentist, and went shopping with us. She even went to church with us. We no longer had to ask cousins or the salesladies in my father's office to go to the movies with us. Nena and I began to enjoy *Aling* Fidela's presence and companionship. She never got angry with us nor ever hit us. But I often saw her spank her own children, and I once saw her beat her nineteen-year old daughter after one of *Aling* Fidela's friends reported having seen the girl coming out of a hotel with her boyfriend.

Despite the closeness and rapport we had with my stepmother, Nena and I never hugged nor kissed her. We never thought of her as a mother, only as a companion. We did not want her to supplant our mother's or *Tía* Emilia's love. *Aling* Fidela, for her part, never sought it either.

My father was usually a very thrifty man. He took pains to economize at every opportunity and said he wanted all members of his family to do likewise. My father was pleased with *Aling* Fidela's frugality. After her marriage, she continued to wear modest and simple cotton dresses. I do remember one instance when I saw my father get very angry with *Aling* Fidela for her "extravagance." Just before the watermelon season, she paid ten pesos for a very large watermelon when the minimum daily wage for a laborer was four pesos.

Another instance where my father overruled *Aling* Fidela was over our first encounter with television. The first Asian games in 1954 were being broadcast live on television. Stores that sold the bulky 30-inch "black boxes with live pictures" attracted crowds outside their windows. People were amazed to see that while our president was speaking in Malacanang Palace, we could see and hear him at the same time.

My stepmother decided to accept an offer from a television salesman: a free two week trial at home. They would bring the box to our house, connect it to house current, set it up with a rabbit-ears antenna and if after a two week period she was not happy with it, she could return it. She chose the two week offer to coincide with the Asian games.

Every night, we went to her house to watch the black-and-white television box. All lights were turned off to see the scenes of the athletic events being beamed from abroad. We were plagued by current interruptions. The fuzzy reception moved vertically constantly and needed constant manual adjustments. The pictures flickered in and out. But we sat there mesmerized for hours on end.

In between athletic events, we saw Hopalong Cassidy while he was still a young man, appearing in western garb, riding horses and chasing the bad guys, along with other western cowboys like Gene Autry and Roy Rodgers and Dale Evans. Our favorite was the Lone Ranger and his Indian sidekick Tonto.

Where normally we talked at night, now all we did was turn off the lights and turn on the television set. My father felt owning a set was a waste of time and bad for the eyes. He only listened to the radio when the news was announced. My father's opinion prevailed, of course, so after the two week trial period, my stepmother had to return the television set to the store.

Had *Aling* Fidela not been a businesswoman, she would probably have spent her time playing mahjongg, as many Filipino wives did. However, she worked very hard. Not being satisfied with her food business in Quiapo, she opened a toy, office and school supplies store in downtown Manila where there was a lot of foot traffic. She rented space across the largest toy store in Manila so that her store received all the overflow traffic of the toy store across the street during the crowded Christmas shopping season.

I enjoyed going to her store because she also stocked paperback books, known then as "pocketbooks." Among my favorites were the Perry Mason mysteries written by Erle Stanley Gardner. I got to take home one book each day, finished reading it overnight, then returned it to her store without having to pay for it. I made sure I did not crease nor mark the pages of the book so that it still could be sold as new.

My father was very proud of *Aling* Fidela's business acumen. I, too, was impressed by her financial success. Even though I was only twelve, since I never spent my weekly allowance, it had accumulated to a fairly substantial amount. One day in 1948, when I was 12 years old, my stepmother asked me if I would be interested in investing in one of her businesses. She guaranteed I would double my money within a few months. By then I had already saved around 500 pesos (about $250.00 US at that time). I gave her my money and, sure enough, after a few months it had grown to 1,000 pesos. I was very excited about making more money and continued to lend her my allowance. I did not question how she was accomplishing her financial wizardry. I was just happy with her results.

Then one day, the police came to our house to question *Aling* Fidela. It seemed that she was lending money at very high interest rates, against usury laws. A dissatisfied customer, who had previously enjoyed borrowing money without any questions asked, reported her to the police. In other words, at twelve years of age, I had doubled my allowance by investing in a loan shark operation. Had it not been for my father's political influence, *Aling* Fidela would have landed in jail. I did not lose my savings of (by then) 2,000 pesos, but she had to promise to the authorities and to my father that she would stop lending money. It also put a stop to the phenomenal growth of my savings.

Aling Fidela also began to change my father. She awakened in my father the desire to go to parties and dances. I had never seen him go out at night before his marriage to her. They frequently went out in the evening, although neither of them smoked, drank, nor gambled, habits that were common in the Philippines. But I understood for the first time the degree of my stepmother's influence when a large formal dinner-dance was held at the luxurious Manila Hotel for her daughter Rita's eighteenth birthday. It was the custom then of people with money to give a coming-out party, a debut, for their daughters' eighteenth birthday.

Four hundred guests, the women dressed in semi-formal attire (ankle-length as opposed to floor-length ball gowns and new for this occasion), and the men in suits, jammed the dance floor of the Manila Hotel one hot night in April. They danced the mambo and the samba to the music of the most popular bandleaders of the time and his orchestra, and enjoyed the seven-course dinner served by white-attired waiters.

I never asked my father how much this all cost, but I knew it was a lot. It seemed to me out of character for him to have given such a lavish party, which ordinarily he would have considered a waste of money. But I did not say anything. Some of my relatives did drop hints about the extravagance of the party, especially for "someone who was not his daughter."

Rita's birthday party created a precedent. Soon, the two other daughters of *Aling* Fidela turned eighteen, and of course, they also had to have dinner-dances in their honor. Then it was Nena who turned eighteen. She had a beautiful party. We all got new formal gowns designed by an up-and-coming young designer, Pitoy Moreno. He eventually became one of the top designers in Asia. I still own many of the dresses and ball gowns he designed for us during that period. By then I already knew how to dance so that I enjoyed myself.

Nena at her debut

When my turn to have a party came, I made a bargain with my father. Instead of spending all that money on a party, why not send me on a trip to the United States. I had always wanted to see America, especially after hearing all about it from my older brothers and sister. My father consented, provided Nena accompany me, and that instead of touring, we would go to college. That's how I came to the USA.

At first, I believed *Aling* Fidela was very frugal, worked herself to the bone, succeeded in business, and cared about my father and his children. However, as I grew older, I learned more and more about her dishonesty, and discovered that much of the image she built up for us was based on lies. I was devastated.

In order to win our acceptance, she lied about any money my father spent on her and her family. In our naïveté, Nena and I believed her. Also, Nena and I were at the age where we were hungry for companionship that she and her daughters provided. We felt betrayed when she convinced my father to build a brand new, expensive house in a nice suburb of Manila for her and her family. To prevent us from questioning the expense, she lied about paying for the house herself. We continued to live in the Vision Street house that had slowly been deteriorating as needed repairs were ignored.

CHAPTER 23
The Church

WHILE IN MY TEENS, I LONGED TO GO TO A CATHOLIC SCHOOL run by nuns, but my father would not allow it. He objected vehemently to our getting a Catholic education, fearing that, under their influence, we would join the sisters' orders. It would have broken his heart if Nena or I had become a nun. It was then common for one daughter of a Catholic family to join an order. My father told us years later that, under the terms of his will, we would be disinherited if we became nuns.

My *Tía* Emilia was a very pious woman. She took over our religious upbringing even though my father was not a Catholic and was so anti-clerical. I only assume my aunt must have set this as a condition for taking care of us. I recollect family evening prayers at around 6:00 pm in front of a large framed replica of the Virgin Mary flanked by two candles.

Before the war, my aunt attended Mass every morning. Once the war came and she could no longer drive there due to the gasoline shortage, she went less often. After the war, my aunt went to church every Friday and Sunday. My aunt attended Friday Mass quite early in the morning, and so we children didn't have to go with her then.

Every Sunday morning, I woke up to the sound of *Inay's* voice giving orders to the servants to wake us up and dress us for church. On Sundays, we did not eat breakfast until after Mass. The start of the car engine meant that it was time to leave for Mass. My aunt patronized only one church, the Quiapo Church. I say "patronized" because nobody went to his parish church. People shopped around and attended the church of their choice. My *Tía* Emilia went to Quiapo because she knew the priest there and because she played cards with the niece of the priest, Blanca.

The Quiapo Church our family attended

In church, I sat through Mass, mesmerized by the flickering candles and hypnotized by the haunting Gounod's *Ave Maria* sung by a soloist of the choir. Her soprano voice would reverberate through the church and give me goose pimples. *Inay* would always nudge me to look straight at the altar instead of looking back at the soloist singing.

I loved to squint my eyes to stare at the twinkling flames of the candles while I daydreamed or prayed the Rosary. I strained my head to smell the incense in the direction of the acolyte waving the censer from side to side as the Mass ended. I enjoyed watching the priests, wearing green, purple, or gold vestments over their white cassocks, genuflecting, standing with their hands upright, and singing the Mass in Latin. I loved listening to the singing. But I never paid attention to the sermon, which was often delivered in Tagalog. Sometimes, in churches located in upper class neighborhoods, the priests delivered their sermons in Spanish. But no matter what language was used, I never listened to the sermon.

As we got older, we were deemed ready to receive the Holy Communion. I don't remember getting prepared for and celebrating my first Holy Communion as others have done. But before we could receive the wafer, we had to confess all our sins. The priests at the confessional booth terrorized me. The old Dominican friars tended to be impatient and unforgiving. Not having received any formal instruction on Catholicism, I had problems deciding what sins to confess. Luckily, Nena went first, and told me her sins and penance. Based on the penance she received, I would confess accordingly. I sometimes made up sins just so I could confess. But later on, Nena and I fought frequently enough that I never had to invent what to say during Confession.

Before I learned to read, *Inay* taught me how to pray in Spanish and in Tagalog. Afterwards, I read from my English/Tagalog Missal during Mass. But I loved hearing the Mass in Latin best. It was so melodic. Afterwards I would always say that Mass in Latin was meant to be sung, something I had heard adults say.

After Mass, we would come out from the church into the plaza, which was filled with food vendors. The fires from the wood-burning clay ovens lit the haggard faces of the old women cooking as well as the hungry people coming out of Mass. The smell of the melting native cheeses and grated coconut spread over the cakes enticed us, along with the crowds exiting the church, to buy and eat the cakes as soon as they were out of the fire. I can still taste the sweet delicious *bibingka* (rice cake) and feel the burn on my tongue as I bit into it.

Inay's friend Blanca was the niece of the parish priest of the Quiapo Church. It was rumored that she was his daughter. She worked at the church. One of her duties included collecting money from the parishioners during the offering. Because it was very common for church pastors to assign to very beautiful young women the task of collecting money from the parishioners, churchgoers at Quiapo were often surprised to see this 45-year-old spinster, dressed unfashionably in an ankle-length dress, black hair swept back and tied, wearing no make-up on her pale face, narrow lips, and rimless glasses atop a pinched nose, approach with the collection plate.

Blanca played mahjongg with *Inay* every afternoon at my aunt's house. Blanca loved to play the Chinese tile game. Win or lose, she was there every afternoon except Sundays. It was a small stakes game. I enjoyed watching *Inay* and her friends laughing and chatting while playing mahjongg.

Blanca was a favorite of mine. Whenever she would leave the table to go to the bathroom, she would let me build her mahjongg wall, throw the dice, break the walls, arrange the tiles according to suit, and sometimes even let me discard the first tile. She was very patient with me, answered my questions, and taught me strategies on how to play the game. She was a good player and often won, taking home her winnings plus the house pot. The sound of mahjongg tiles hitting against each other always brings back to me those happy childhood memories.

Once, while Blanca was in the bathroom and *Inay* was preparing the *merienda* in the kitchen, I listened in on the conversation between the mahjongg ladies.

"Elsa, have you heard the news about Blanca?" Mrs. Fuentes, the lady whose whole body jiggled when she laughed, asked the woman on her right, a pretty woman in her thirties, a contemporary of my cousin Grading.

"No, what is it?"

"She has a boyfriend, a good looking young man, apparently much younger than our Blanca." Mrs. Fuentes spoke in a whisper while glancing at the bathroom door.

"Who told you?" asked Elsa as she started arranging her wall.

I was quietly building up Blanca's wall with my ears at attention. I hoped the two ladies wouldn't notice my presence and stop talking.

"I met her landlady at the market yesterday. We talked for a while, and when I mentioned that I knew one of her boarders, Blanca, she started to tell me all about her boyfriend."

"How come she hasn't told us? We've been playing mahjongg with her for years."

"I don't know. She may be keeping him under wraps because he's much younger than she is. He comes in a taxi and picks her up. They don't return until late in the night, according to her landlady."

"Shhh. Blanca's coming. Let's talk later. I'll share a *calesa* with you."

Blanca returned to the mahjongg table and in a joking manner, said, "I hope you ladies have not been talking about me." She laughed and patted my head as I stood up to yield her my seat.

The two ladies looked at each other and smiled. They started to play when *Inay* returned from the kitchen carrying a tray of soft drinks and rice cakes. For me, one of the best parts of the mahjongg game was to partake of the sweets during the *merienda* break. If I sat quietly during the game, I would be allowed one sweet treat.

At the Quiapo Church, the pews were so crowded it was always "standing room only." Thanks to my aunt's friendship with Blanca, we sat in a special section near the altar, on padded velvet seats, in front of the communion railing. These seats were reserved for visiting prelates and other VIPs. Every Friday and Sunday morning at 8 o'clock, my aunt, sister Nena, and I would walk up to the altar and take our reserved seats. We were above the crowd, the noise, and the sweating churchgoers. This was the way to pray to God.

Quiapo Church has on its main altar a black Jesus of Nazareth, kneeling while carrying the Cross. Black Jesus is the patron saint of Quiapo. January 9th was the feast day of the black Jesus, and every house in Quiapo celebrated the day by having a fiesta. Thousands of baby suckling pigs, fattened for this occasion, were killed and roasted over open fires. Housewives, with the help of servants, prepared great quantities of tangy sauce to accompany the *lechon*, roast pig, boiled white rice, fresh fruit salads, caramel custard, and assorted native cakes that were served to invited as well as uninvited guests. The occasional sound of plates crashing, glasses tinkling, and music playing could be heard from house to house. Young people came to dance the latest steps; old people sat down to eat and gossip.

The procession of the statue of Jesus of Nazareth was the main event. It started from the church plaza and followed the narrow streets of the district. Hundreds of penitents carried on their towel-draped shoulders the makeshift wooden altar, adorned with green *ilang-ilang* and white *sampaguita*, bearing Jesus and his Cross along the various streets of Quiapo. The men moved in unison, and their leader barked instructions to coordinate their movements. One year, the statue had slipped from its base and fallen, crushing some people to death. Afterward, they took extra care so as not to repeat the tragedy. Hundreds of thousands of the faithful lined the route of the procession at a safe distance, praying and singing.

That year, the Friday before the feast, as Inay, Nena, and I were seated in our special section in church, Blanca, looking unusually pretty and happy, passed by with the collection plate. She winked at me as I dropped a peso bill on her plate. That was the last time I saw her. On January 10th, my aunt, sister, and I walked up the altar of Quiapo church to take our usual reserved seats. But as we approached the pew, an acolyte informed us that the seats were no longer available to us. It seemed that Blanca disappeared with the church collection after the Mass of the Feast of the black Jesus of Nazareth. Neither my aunt nor the mahjongg ladies ever saw or heard from her again.

CHAPTER 24
Movies

FILIPINOS LOVE GOING TO THE MOVIES. During the war, this became a favorite form of escape from the hardships of life. After the war, we would pass by several movie houses on the way to school, and so we knew in advance which movies we would be given permission to see. My brothers and I would stop to look at the still photos of scenes from the movies being shown. I loved to linger in front of theaters, especially at midday, to feel and smell the cold air coming from the lobby. At that time, theaters were the only air-conditioned public buildings.

Two glass-enclosed ticket booths, staffed by women and flanked by armed policemen, stood at each corner of the entrance. After the war, another sign, in addition to the list of prices of admission, appeared outside the ticket booth: "Deposit firearms here." Filipinos were apt to carry their guns everywhere. Before this precaution was instituted, several gunfights occurred inside theaters.

Theater lobbies were wide, open, and two stories tall, topped by a crystal chandelier. Standing inside the cool lobby, I could sometimes hear the dialogue spoken in the movies being shown. Two ushers in uniforms with braids and epaulets on their shoulders stood at attention at the foot of two grand staircases leading to the choice balcony and loge seats. The ushers also collected tickets from the orchestra patrons. Philippine landscape scenes or the faces of famous actors and actresses were painted by local artists on the tall side walls along the staircases. A dark maroon velvet curtain separated the lobby from the entrance to the orchestra section, which was set far back into the building.

During the war, American films were no longer available locally, but one nearby theater showing second-run movies somehow still had copies of the *Flash Gordon* series. It did not matter that the seats had bedbugs or the place smelled of urine. It was still a treat for me to be taken by my two brothers to watch Flash Gordon every week, hanging onto the suspense of how Flash Gordon would get out of his latest predicament.

Later on in the war, many of the theaters closed for lack of films to show. Some converted to live vaudeville acts in Tagalog. I remember one particular vaudeville show that featured two famous bald Filipino comic actors. From the balcony seats, I saw a brightly-lit stage, resembling a small Philippine village with *nipa* huts in the foreground and rice fields painted on a cloth screen as a background. The catchy sound of Filipino folk tunes came from a small band. The townspeople were making preparations for a *barrio fiesta* (small town feast).

The two comic actors, dressed like Japanese soldiers, were performing a skit about the occupation of a rural village. They mimicked the manner Japanese soldiers shouted their orders to the natives, authoritatively demanding that everyone bow to them. The realistic scene provoked the loudest laughter when one of the actors portraying a Japanese soldier boasted to his comrade of his recent take of confiscated watches. He pulled up his sleeve to show watches from his wrist up to his shoulder. The audience howled with laughter at the sight of the wristwatches because it was so true to life. Japanese soldiers were apt to confiscate wristwatches from Filipinos for no reason.

The crowd's clapping and roar brought down the house. I had never heard such thunderous applause before. But the Japanese censors soon put an end to the show. They closed down the act as well as the theater. That was the end of my vaudeville entertainment. The two actors were jailed but later released, going on to enjoy a successful career after the war portraying Japanese soldiers in Filipino films.

Tía Sisang's youngest daughter Piling, seven years my senior, was often my and Nena's companion at the movies as soon as the war ended. Piling loved going to the movies, and she selected what we saw. My knowledge of English at the time was almost nil, and the classic movies Piling chose were a blur to me (until much later, when I had a chance to see them again). Piling enjoyed films such as *Spellbound* with Ingrid Bergman and Gregory Peck and *Gentlemen's Agreement* with Gregory Peck and Dorothy McGuire. We never missed any of Ingrid Bergman's films. But since Piling liked dramas and hated musicals, until I met *Aling* Fidela's daughters, I never saw a musical.

Unfortunately for my sister Nena and me, Piling was nearsighted and had to sit very close to the screen. Since the theaters were usually crowded, our seats were almost always in the fourth row from the front and way to the left of the screen. I had a very distorted view of Ingrid Bergman's face.

Going to the movies was my favorite pastime, next to reading, during the late 1940s and early 1950s. Each movie house showed only the movies from one studio. MGM pictures were shown at the Ideal Theater, Warner Brothers at the Lyric, Twentieth-Century at Rizal, Universal Pictures at the Times, Columbia Pictures at the Life, RKO pictures at the Capitol, Paramount at Avenue Theater, etc. I still can remember in which theatre I saw all the MGM musicals with Jane Powell, Kathryn Grayson, and Judy Garland. I saw Rita Hayworth at the Life, and Maria Montes, Yvonne de Carlo, and Deanna Durbin at the Times. American movies were never dubbed, nor did they provide subtitles. It was assumed that all Filipinos could understand English.

Filipinos were notoriously noisy inside the theaters, with incessant conversations, frequent munching of nuts and chestnuts, and a lot of hooting and booing, depending on the type of movie. Peanut vendors walked up and down the aisles, calling out the merits of their wares. I always bought a small, heart-shaped, clear bag of cashews, which cost 25 centavos. During chestnut season, I bought a half-kilo of boiled chestnuts to peel and eat at the movies. I threw the peelings on the floor, just as everyone else did, where they were crunched under people's feet as they walked to their seats.

People entered and left the theater at all times; movies ran continuously, and there were no advertised start times as there are in the United States. You arrived at the theater while a movie was usually already in progress. You then stayed through the end, and continued watching as the movie started up again, and left when the movie got to the point you came in.

After the war, many movies about the Japanese occupation were made by the Philippine movie industry in Tagalog. Some of the movies, showing the hurt and anguish of the Filipinos, fanned anti-Japanese sentiments well into the 1950s. By the time I left Manila in 1954, Japanese ships couldn't dock in Philippine harbors. The ships had to be unloaded by small boats, far away from shore. No Japanese businessman dared show his face in Manila. But the anti-Japanese feeling is gone now. Japanese ships, planes, and cars are everywhere. Filipino entrepreneurs have opened acres and acres of golf courses to lure the Japanese tourists and businessmen. I even spied a street named after a Japanese city.

During my movie going days when I was a child, the main floor cost the cheapest, one peso and twenty centavos. For comparison, the minimum wage for a laborer per day was four pesos. Theaters were usually crowded, so that whenever a popular movie was being shown, we had to pay double for balcony seats or even triple for the loges. People who were on dates often sat in the balcony, way up high near the projection room, in order to kiss and not be seen. I enjoyed seating in the loges because it was quieter, and the seats were comfortable and roomy. The movie houses were open for business from seven in the morning to nine in the evening.

People who wore Army or police uniforms got in free. Priests and nuns were also allowed to enter without paying. At that time, the Catholic Church acted as the National Censor Board, and it banned movies that were not in accord with the teachings of the Church. One such banned movie was *The Outlaw* starring Jane Russell. However, according to the rumors, a lot of priests were seen coming out of the theater where the movie was being shown.

The customs from the movie theaters carried over into church. People came in and out of the Mass as if they were attending a movie. Since Mass was offered hourly during the day, worshipers would drop in at any time and then leave whenever they felt that they had done enough praying or the priest had reached the same part of the Mass where they came in. For example, if someone came during the *Agnus Dei*, she would stay and pray until the next Mass, then leave when the next priest started praying *Agnus Dei*. There were always people milling about, going in and out, standing up or kneeling. I probably spent most of my time looking around and watching people go by. It was difficult to concentrate or pray.

CHAPTER 25
Miss Philippines 1948

ALTHOUGH WE STILL LIVED IN THE OLD VISION STREET HOUSE with no hot water, as the years after the war progressed, some of my relatives began to display many of the trappings of great wealth. Others fell in income and relied on my father for partial support.

Tío Exequiel was the third oldest son in my father's family. He was in his mid-fifties when I lived in *Tía* Emilia's house next to his. When I think of him, I remember his bald head, rimless glasses, light complexion, special diet because of diabetes, his use of long underwear, and the fact that he had two mistresses simultaneously.

It is a given in Filipino culture that a married man would take on a mistress. But for a widower, the sky was the limit when it came to the number of mistresses. My *Tío* Exequiel was no exception.

His first wife, who belonged to a rich family, died young and left a baby daughter. Teresita was raised by her maternal grandmother and two maiden aunts, Consuelo and Conchita. It had been hoped by the family that *Tío* Exequiel would marry Consuelo, the younger and prettier of the sisters. However, whenever a man got interested in one of them, the other sister would criticize him so much that the sister would lose interest in him. And each sister took turns criticizing the beau of the other. The two women thus remained unmarried, despite their deep desire to get married. Indeed, Consuelo and Conchita were critical of everything.

Once, I happened to have been wearing the same dress on two occasions when we visited my cousin. Consuelo said to me in front of everyone, "Katinka, don't you have any other dress to wear?"

I was too embarrassed to answer.

My uncle, instead of marrying one of the sisters, decided to take on a mistress, Luisa, with whom he started to have children (they ultimately had seven). To make matters worse for him in the eyes of his critical sisters-in-law, he took on a second and younger mistress, Brigida, a cousin of Luisa, at the same time.

Everyone knew his schedule. Even though he made his home with Brigida in the house next to us and eventually had three children with her, lunch and siesta were at *Tía* Luisa's house several blocks away.

Two of his children with Brigida and Luisa were born on the same day. The two women remained on good terms with one another. Their children played with each other. I never heard them fight with one another. The adults in my family never questioned the arrangement, and neither did I. I thought it was normal and common. I probably heard more gossip about Consuelo and Conchita than about Luisa and Brigida.

I was closer to *Tía* Brigida than *Tía* Luisa because she lived next door to us. She must have been ten years younger and a lot slimmer than Luisa. I remember her as being kind and patient. She tolerated our noise when we played in their house, jumped on their bed, and played with her high heels and make-up. I was fascinated with the way she put on her long silk stockings, gently rolling them first and preventing her nails from snagging the stockings. The straightening of the seams behind took just as long. I vowed I'd never wear stockings since it took so long to put them on.

My father felt that Exequiel would end up being the richest of all his brothers. Despite supporting three households, he was even more frugal than my father. He had the same business as my father, import and export. But the comparison ended there. While my father was generous to his relatives, *Tío* Exequiel was not. He used his car only on Sundays; we used ours every day. Although a diabetic and almost blind toward the end of his life, he ended living the longest among all his brothers and sisters.

Tía Sisang was my father's youngest sister. She "did not marry well," according to *Inay*. She was widowed early and left with five children to support. *Tía* Sisang did not wear dresses but instead favored the Philippine costume of a wrapped sarong for a skirt and a loose top. She used no make-up and wore her long hair tied in a bun at the nape of her neck.

Tía Sisang taught me how to use my mother's Singer sewing machine and how to crochet doilies. She carried her thread and crochet hooks in a black and gold cloth bag, always ready to crochet as soon as she was seated on our living room sofa. She only crocheted doilies, which she washed and starched herself. They resembled white butterflies, ready for flight. She told me the secret of why the doilies appeared so: she made the outer edges looser and crocheted more stitches than were necessary. The starch stiffened the outer edges and made them look like they were frozen in mid-air. Since she did not have much money, she gave everyone her crocheted doilies as Christmas presents. This was all she could afford.

My father supplanted her tiny pension by giving her a monthly allowance. In return for my father's kindness, she often came to our house to cook. She was a wonderful cook. Whenever we were without a cook, *Tía* Sisang would willingly come to cook for us in Vision Street. She always cooked for our birthdays. For me, she prepared sticky rice with boiled, sweetened corn kernels.

Had it not been for my father's financial help, she would have had to go into service as a cook, since she did not have much of an education. As it was, there was a time when she served as a cook in *Tía* Emilia's house when we lived there. My father helped her build a small house in La Loma north of Manila, which she shared with her oldest daughter, Leonie, her policeman husband, two grand-children, and *Tía* Sisang's four other children.

Tía Sisang always came to our house on December 28th, *El Dia de los Santos Inocentes*, Innocents' Day, to borrow money from my father. The tradition was that any amount borrowed on this day need not be repaid, as long as you said the word "Innocents' Day" after the lender had given you the money. We always knew what she was up to whenever she knocked on our door on that particular day. But my father obliged her and played the game with her.

I loved *Tía* Sisang dearly. She was fat and jolly. She was much shorter than *Tía* Emilia, plump, freckled, and always wore black because she was a widow. Unlike *Tía* Emilia, she was a very warm person and very cuddly. I remember sitting on her lap and smelling onions and garlic on her clothes.

Unfortunately, like many people, *Tía* Sisang suffered from the fault of favoring one child, the oldest, over everyone else in the family. Our movie companion Piling, *Tia* Sisang's middle child and youngest daughter, could have gone to the university. She was very bright. But despite my father's help, there was not enough money for all five children to go to college. Piling studied optometry instead and eventually married another optometrist.

Piling became estranged from her mother, as well as the rest of the family, when she accused her mother openly of hiring her out as household help and favoring Leonie, her oldest sister. It was true that when she was a teenager, Piling came to work in our house, not really as a servant but almost like a paid companion. This hurt her feelings, and the resentment built up. After she had her own children, she saw how her mother gave preferential treatment to her older grandchildren.

In the eyes of all the relatives, Piling had sinned by openly quarreling with her mother. *Tía* Sisang disowned her, saying she was no longer her daughter and not welcome at her house. We saw very little of Piling after that. There was no reconciliation between the two, each one believing the other wrong. *Tía* Sisang died without forgiving her daughter. None of the relatives could interfere in their quarrel. I felt very sad about this because I believed Piling was right.

My father never tried to show any favoritism. He always told us he loved us all equally, but in my heart I thought I was his favorite. Of course, it is possible that both Nena and Fe felt the same way.

When I was in my early teens, the closest I got to fame, royalty, and what seemed to be a fairy tale life, was when my first cousin Cely was crowned Miss Philippines of 1948. Cely was the daughter of my father's half-brother Cesareo.

A Manila newspaper, to boost circulation, decided to run a Miss Philippines contest. The nominated candidates had to meet certain "beauty standards," but judges would not select the winner; instead, she would be chosen by popular vote. Each issue of the daily newspaper would have a ballot worth ten votes. At the prescribed date, all ballots would be tallied and the candidate with the most votes would be declared Miss Philippines.

Someone sent in a picture of my cousin Cely, then sixteen years old but already very beautiful, and nominated her. First there was surprise among our relatives; then everyone got into the spirit of the contest and started working in earnest for Cely's candidacy. Her parents, *Tío* Zario and *Tía* Diding, at first were concerned that the beauty contest was not "decent." When they learned that, unlike the Miss Universe pageant, the candidate did not have to wear a bathing suit and no body measurements were to be taken, they became her most enthusiastic supporters.

At the time of the beauty contest, my uncle's various businesses were flourishing: a bus company, a string of bowling alleys all over Manila, and an office supply store downtown. The family had moved from a house behind us on Dimasalang Street and built a pink cement mansion with a swimming pool in Caloocan, a suburb of Manila, just a few blocks from the statue "Cry of Balintawak." Their two-hectare estate was ringed with pine trees and a tall iron fence.

Although only sixteen, Cely already looked full-grown. She was five-foot six, slim, had beautiful legs, a dazzling dimpled smile, clear brown eyes, an oval face, and naturally curly brown hair. She could charm anyone with her melodious voice. She looked like her mother except that *Tía* Diding had gained weight in her middle years.

Nobody expected Cely to win. During the weeks before the final balloting, she placed third or fourth. But on the final day, everyone in the family, especially my uncle, submitted so many ballots for Cely that she surpassed the front-runner and won the title of Miss Philippines of 1948. The First Lady of the Philippines crowned Cely during an important fair. Cely was resplendent in a Filipino *terno*, a native evening dress with butterfly sleeves, designed by a famous local couturier. She wore her own diamond tiara handmade in Meycauayan. Her diamond necklace was rumored to be worth hundreds of thousand pesos. The son of the Governor of the

Central Bank of the Philippines, Pete Carmona, her boyfriend, escorted her to all the festivities.

My father and all his children were invited to all the parties, both at the time of the crowning and afterwards. I remember these visits to *Tío* Zario's house as a series of weekend dances and midnight swims. Even though Nena and I were just starting our teens and had not learned how to dance yet, we enjoyed being invited to Christmas and other parties at their house. I remember the festive atmosphere at the house: multi-colored light bulbs hanging near the swimming pool area and decorating the pine trees, the sumptuous buffet table laid out for dinner after Midnight Mass, the joyous and infectious laughter of my uncle and aunt, my aunt decked out in the latest fashion and wearing the largest diamonds I had ever laid eyes on, and the cute young men and women guests dancing to the Glen Miller records and latest Patti Paige and Doris Day hits.

Within a year, Cely was married to Pete Carmona. It was the fairy tale wedding of the year. The father of the groom, as is the custom in the Philippines, paid for all wedding expenses, including the honeymoon. The bride's father gave them a fully furnished house as a wedding present, together with a cook and a maid, since my cousin didn't know her way around the kitchen. My *Tía* Diding gave her daughter some of her emerald and diamond jewelry.

The wedding was celebrated at the Manila Cathedral by the Bishop of Manila. A thousand invitees filled the Cathedral, overwhelming the small parking lot of the church by all the chauffeur-driven cars of the guests. Hundreds of curiosity-seekers loitered outside, to gawk at and admire the wedding party and their well-dressed and bejeweled guests. Private police guards wearing pistols were posted inside and outside the Cathedral to prevent any disturbance. The wedding march was played by a concert pianist friend of the bride, and the soloist at the Mass was a famous opera singer, hired by the family of the groom. I sat in the pew, overwhelmed with emotion and the grandeur of the occasion. I had never, before or since, been a witness to such a wedding.

Fairy tales are supposed to have happy endings, but unfortunately the story of Cely ended tragically. The couple had two children, but the marriage ended in "divorce, Philippine style." That meant a separation with no chance of a remarriage, which was only possible after obtaining a divorce abroad (divorce was not available in the Philippines at that time).

My *Tío* Zario suffered a heart attack not long afterward and died, leaving my *Tía* Diding and his oldest son Cesar to manage a heavily mortgaged empire. Soon, the fleet of buses became one, the bowling alleys had to be sold, and the import-export business was sold to the highest bidder. Eventually, everything collapsed when some relatives took advantage of their lack of business acumen. My aunt had to sell her jewelry at a loss and move to smaller quarters. My *Tía* died soon after, a sad and disillusioned woman. Cesar ended up driving a taxi in one of the southern islands, and Cely became impoverished, her beauty gone. It was a very sad ending for a once happy, prosperous family.

CHAPTER 26

My Father's First Stroke

I STILL REMEMBER THE DAY MY FATHER HAD HIS STROKE. It was in 1950; I was fourteen. We were spending Sunday afternoon at my stepmother's house. My stepmother's son was recounting the story of the movie *The Beast with Five Fingers,* acting out the movement of the severed hand playing on the piano keys, then reaching toward us as if to grab us.

Our screams and shrieks prevented us from hearing my stepmother, who was in the living room with my father. She was crying and calling out his name. Right before her eyes, my father started to lose his power of speech and began feeling numb on his left side. She did not know what to do. She sent someone to get a doctor. When we realized what was happening, we rushed to the living room to see her setting a warm iron on my father's left arm, the one that had gone numb, to see whether he could feel it. She could have caused second-degree burns had she not been stopped.

After what seemed like an eternity, a doctor and an ambulance came and took my father to the Philippine General Hospital. Anyone who has witnessed a loved one being taken away by ambulance to a hospital will understand how I must have felt. I was helpless and scared, not knowing whether my father would live.

My sister and I were allowed to visit him the next day, but he was still in a coma. We cried all night; we did not know what would happen to us if my father died. By this time, *Tía* Emilia had been dead for a couple of years. Even though we were in good terms with our stepmother then, we knew her first priorities were her own children.

All my life, I had been terrified of my father dying and leaving us orphans. Now it seemed as if my worst fears were coming true. Little did I realize at the time that the consequences of his death would have been even worse than I imagined. In the Philippines, orphaned children often ended up as virtual servants in the houses of their relatives, under the guise of charity. It did not matter if their parents had money. If my father had died then, my sister and I would never have seen an inheritance. As young as we were, other relatives would have moved in on our father's business empire and taken it over. Nena and I really had no one except each other. Our older brothers and sister were studying in the United States and couldn't come home.

Everything seemed so black during that period. It was like a dark, starless winter night, when sunrise is very slow in coming, sometimes not even showing itself. My feelings of sadness and anguish resembled the deepest purple of a sunrise, when the sun is not yet out.

My father endured a slow and long recovery. He was in the hospital for months under the care of two cardiologists and a private nurse. One came to check up on him during the morning hours, while the other one came at night. The medical visits continued even after he came home.

The morning doctor was an up-and-coming young bachelor, physician also to the President of the Philippines, Elpidio Quirino. My stepmother had her eye on him for her eldest daughter, Rita. Rita was the opposite of the ideal of Filipina womanhood. Relatives warned us not to associate with her. While my father was hospitalized due to the stroke and my stepmother stayed in the hospital with him, Aling Fidela's three daughters stayed in our home with us to "keep us company." At night, Rita's boyfriend would arrive surreptitiously at our house (I heard him come in), stay overnight, and leave before dawn so that the neighbors wouldn't see him.

When Dr. Tangco came to our house to examine my father on a weekend, my father and stepmother would ask Dr. Tangco to stay longer for some refreshments and listen to Rita sing one of Jeanette McDonald's favorite songs. Rita had been taking voice lessons and had a fairly good voice. Dr. Tangco was too polite to refuse the musical treat. Eventually my father's condition improved and no longer required the services of a doctor in the morning. Thus ended my stepmother's unsuccessful attempt at matchmaking.

The internist who visited my father at home in the evenings was Dr. Austria. His beautiful, young second wife always accompanied him on his night visits, but she always waited inside their car. She could never be persuaded by either my father or stepmother to come into the house. Dr. Austria's first wife had become seriously ill during World War II while Dr. Austria was doing his residency in a New York hospital. The war prevented him from coming home, and he only found out she had died upon his return. She left two young children.

Eventually, my father was walking again with the help of a cane and talking almost normally. I felt great relief. It reminded me of the sky's appearance at sunrise, when the sun is peeking out of the horizon, when the dark background of the sky changed color, from dark purple to deep orange, light purple, and pink, as if the sky had burst into flames. What a joy!

His recuperation continued. There were daily trips to the hot springs in Los Baños, Laguna, about an hour's drive from our house. He eventually relearned to move his paralyzed limbs again. The effects of the stroke on his speech gradually diminished so that he could speak normally. The chauffeur Macario became my father's right-hand man after the stroke. Macario became his legs. Besides driving him to Laguna, he did errands for my father and helped my father walk. He enabled him to continue to run his businesses during his recuperation. He was one of the most faithful, loyal employees we ever had. I was glad to hear that my brothers provided him with a good pension until his death.

CHAPTER 27

We Children Leave Home

OVER TIME, MY FATHER SAW FRICTION DEVELOPING between my oldest sister Fe, my brother Vic, and my stepmother. It was time for them to attend college, so he sent Fe and Vic abroad to study. Fe and Vic and two cousins left on a freighter bound for San Francisco in 1948, the last ship to stop in Shanghai before the city fell to the Chinese Communists. Fe and Vic ended up meeting their future spouses in the United States.

Meanwhile, my oldest brother, Eddy, who had developed tuberculosis, was sent to one of my father's farms to get some fresh air, good food, and recover from his illness. He not only recovered but also fell in love with the daughter of the farm's caretaker, Inez.

As before, words of disapproval came from some of our female relatives because Inez came from a "lower class." Some also criticized her for being dark and for speaking Tagalog with an accent. But my father only asked them if they loved each other, and, when he was satisfied with their answers, gave them his blessing.

Eddy and Inez were married in her hometown and moved in with us until they could find an apartment. They occupied the only double bed in our house in Vision Street. My father and stepmother, who had been using the bed, had to move to our bedroom temporarily and slept on the floor. The crowding eased after Eddy and Inez moved to a rented house across from his mother's house

(Mamá Carmen, my father's second wife) on Oroquieta Street in Manila.

My first trip back to the Philippines in nearly half a century recently occurred when I was invited to Eddy and Inez's 50th wedding anniversary. They have ten children. The official photographer for the anniversary had to take two different shots of the wedding party because of the number of people involved, over a hundred in all: ten children, numerous sons- and daughters-in-law, grandchildren, and great grandchildren. A panoramic picture may not even have sufficed to include them all.

My brothers Vic (left) and Paking (right)

A year after Vic and Fe went away, it was Paking's turn to go to the United States to study. He had to wait until he was fourteen in order to travel unaccompanied on a plane. He almost did not make it because the Pan American Clipper, bound for San Francisco, with stops in Hong Kong, Tokyo, and Honolulu, had engine problems and had to delay its departure. Paking laughed and made jokes about the plane while we were waiting for it to be repaired. Although perspiring profusely, Paking showed no fear when it was time to board. He was the first in our family to fly. Two passengers were paged repeatedly before the airline concluded that they were not going to show up for this particular flight. To anyone who cared to listen, my father recounted the story of Paking's courage in boarding a plane that had been grounded for engine problems when two grown men opted not to take the same plane.

Paking finished high school in a private preparatory school near Pittsburgh, Pennsylvania. He went on to study Business at Amherst College and received an MBA from Stanford University at the age of 21. He met and married a Filipina born in Hawaii.

About this time, Nena and I were at the University of the Philippines. I became a reluctant candidate for the U. P. Student Council. Nena became my campaign manager and helped me to win a seat. I did not want to run, politics and public speaking not being my fortes. However, the sorority I belonged to, Sigma Delta Lambda, and its ally, Upsilon Sigma Phi fraternity, needed a U. P. High School graduate with good grades to complete its slate of candidates for the Student Council. So I was drafted to run for office.

Without Nena, I would not have gotten any votes. She did all the campaigning, dragging me from classroom to classroom, introducing me, and urging fellow students to vote for me. I stood in front of each classroom and forced a smile. Her introductions were longer than my speeches.

I thought I'd die when I had to stand and speak on the stage of the University Theater in front of all four thousand of the male students in the ROTC program in order to urge them to vote for me. I don't know if the ROTC students noticed my shaking legs and quivering voice as I gave my name and major. Fortunately, there was a microphone to amplify my timid pleas.

I was elected, seventh among eight Student Council members from the College of Liberal Arts. My first introduction to Philippine politics came when we, as newly-elected members, were "kidnapped" and hidden from the opposition party by our own party, to ensure the party's forming a majority to elect the President of the Student Council. When I became distressed, I was told this was a routine practice done every year to prevent the opposition from circumventing the results of the elections.

I eventually overcame my shyness and learned to speak in front of a crowd when I was in my thirties, by then married with children. I have to thank my membership in the League of Women Voters for this.

The SS President Wilson

When I was 18, my father sent my sister Nena and me to study in the United States. By then, he had fully recovered from his illness. In June 1954, Nena and I sailed for San Francisco on the SS President Wilson. We were bound for the International House at the University of California, Berkeley, where we would live for several years and complete our education.

At the time, I held strong anti-Japanese sentiments because I blamed them for the death of so many people, including my brother Hiram, and for the suffering we endured during the war. This terrible prejudice might have continued further into my adulthood were it not for what happened to us after we stopped in Honolulu.

Two Japanese teenagers came to share our first class cabin for four. Had we booked a later sailing as planned, we would have had a cabin for two. But my brother Paking had cabled us from San Francisco to come earlier. He was getting married and wanted us to be there. So the only cabin we could get was one for four people. We were reassured that during the twenty-one days of travel time, we would have roommates only during the last five days.

At first, Nena and I were furious and ignored the Japanese girls. But, sharing a room, it only took one day before we began to talk about our common interests, which we found to be many. They were visiting relatives in California while we were on our way to Berkeley to study. We began to eat and do all the shipboard activities together. Before they came on board, we had no young people to spend time with because most of the passengers were much older than we were.

Katinka and Nena aboard the SS President Wilson

In four short days, I forgot the war and my hatred. I realized it was not the fault of these girls that our two countries had been at war. With friendship and personal contact, my anger and hate melted away. This was an important lesson I was never to forget.

During my studies at Berkeley, I was to meet people from all over the world. I ended up marrying a South American, living in the American Midwest, and eventually traveling to and living in many corners of the world.

Sergio and Katinka Rodriguez: On their wedding day
in 1959 (left) and in Berkeley, CA in 1997 (right)

My husband's work as a physicist brought me into contact with people of many nationalities. Among them were many Japanese scientists and their wives, whom we frequently entertained as guests in our home. To reciprocate, many of them invited us to visit them in Japan. We have been to Japan several times, and I have made many friends there. My life has become immeasurably richer since I opened my heart and ceased to hold on to hatred and old grudges.

CHAPTER 28

Remembering

AFTER A YEAR IN BERKELEY, I RECEIVED NEWS that my father had suffered a series of strokes, was hospitalized again, and was not expected to live long. I remembered my father's admonition when Nena and I sailed: not to return home unless we had finished school. I wanted to rush to his side, but I wanted reassurance I would not be scolded. I dreaded my father's wrath at seeing me at his bedside when he recovered consciousness, almost more than the fear that I would not see him alive again. In the end, I did return home from the United States and was able to spend some time with him before he died.

My father died in May, the same month my mother died. Even though I was only twenty-one years old at the time, my stay in the United States had given me independence, and I had learned to accept death's inevitability. I felt I had conquered my fear of death.

After my father's death, I attended the reading of the will following his funeral. I noticed how differently *Aling* Fidela acted. All the years she had been my stepmother, she had had an attitude of humility and subservience. Suddenly, it was all gone. My sister Nena and I were crying, but she was dry-eyed and insistent that she get the substantial inheritance to which she felt she was entitled.

I was furious and did not try to seek out any further contact with her. It seemed that she was also not interested in spending any more time with the girls who had once been her constant companions, and so we lost touch. Over the years, I did hear news about her occasionally. When she was in her late seventies, the family gossip was that she was living with a young dance instructor. She had always loved to dance. The last news I heard of her was that when she died, much to the chagrin of her children, *Aling* Fidela left the bulk of her estate to the dance instructor.

I loved my father and would have done anything for him. My respect and love for my father is combined with a deep fear of him. While growing up, I feared displeasing him and being punished, and I also greatly feared letting him down by not succeeding. I also feel anger at how complicated our lives were. I disliked his womanizing and all of the women and children that he brought into our family. I respect him for providing for all the children he fathered, but many times I longed for a more "normal" life.

I admire my father for his success, his "rags to riches story." However, my father was a very thrifty man. It offended his nature to buy luxurious goods or splurge on possessions, and he wanted all members of his family to do the same. He frowned on ostentation. The only luxury he allowed for himself and his family was a car and his driver, Macario. After he became successful in business after the war, we still continued to occupy the small house in Vision Street.

When I was in my teens, I could never understand why we lived in such crowded conditions after the war ended. I assumed we were not poor because we had a car with a chauffeur, the only car in the neighborhood at that time. But he refused to move to a larger and better house. That same house was labeled "a slum" by my new sister-in-law when she arrived from the United States with my brother Vic. They came to stay with my father and stepmother in the mid-fifties until they could find a house. This sister-in-law's working class parents in Oakland, California owned a much nicer house than my father, who by then was a millionaire.

In contrast, my father's generosity to others was legendary. Anyone who came to him to ask for money received help. Although he was anti-clerical, he was sympathetic to the various orders of Catholic sisters who came routinely to his office, seeking monetary contributions. During my teenage years, I saw a pair of nuns coming out of his office more than once. I would tease him, "I thought you were anti-Catholic," and he would reply, "I have nothing against nuns personally. They are so poor and work hard. They need help."

He was very active in his Masonic Lodge, where he reached the 33rd degree. He single-handedly saved his local chapter of the Masonic Lodge from bankruptcy by donating a vast sum of money to the organization, something I found out only at my father's funeral during the course of a Mason's eulogy.

In my father's time, a man was the absolute ruler of his home and his family. We were not allowed any freedom. In a way, we were prisoners, caged by love and authority. I wanted to be sent to America, both to see the world and to escape the drudgery of life at home: the petty social life at school, the crowdedness of our small house, the boredom and sameness of our daily routine, and the suffocating clasp of my father's control.

It is harder for me to write about my mother. How do you write about someone you never met nor saw? I have so many questions. How did she feel about waking up each morning? Did she like to read or write? Did she enjoy cooking, sewing, reading? What were her dreams for herself? What were her dreams for her children? What made her laugh? What made her cry? Who chose our names, she or my father? Did she have any musical talent? Nena sings, Paking plays the piano well, and I am a photographer and writer. My father said he had no one in his family that had musical or artistic talent. Could these talents have come from her?

The only things I have of my mother are a few pictures. I look at a photograph of her as a young woman. She is very pretty, but she is a stranger to me. I don't recall her voice, and no one has told me that I sound like her. It seems to me that my living relatives have forgotten her. I was too uncaring about my personal history when the people who were close to my mother were still alive. All I have left with me now are questions, but sadly there's no one to answer them.

Children grow up and accept their world as normal. I have lived now for over forty years in a small town in Indiana, in an environment about as far removed from my childhood world as is possible. For many years, I contrasted the deprivation of my life as a child with the material comfort of life in the United States and felt relieved to have escaped the supposed poverty of my youth. As a child growing up in war-torn Manila, I saw the United States as Shangri-La, the paradise where all good things were possible. The Philippines of my childhood, in contrast, seemed shabby and unpleasant.

It was only after I had lived in Indiana for many years that I came to appreciate the incredible richness of the world I lived in as a child, the intricate texture of life lived close to the bone, skin to skin with family members; the wealth of ideas and stories amidst poverty, deprivation and death, the jewels hidden under the pettiness, conventionality and crowding. Growing up in Indiana, my daughters had no such wealth. They grew up alone, isolated in their large, white rooms, missing without even realizing it the constant companionship of family, the inevitable storytelling, the fables and morals constantly living themselves out around me. I learned early on about loss and betrayal, about grasping for wealth and how it stunts people, how bad habits can unravel any hope of success.

Sergio, Katinka, Cecilia and Katrin Rodriguez visiting Sergio's mother Berta Fontannaz in Chile in the 1960s

Seen from the viewpoint of my American daughters, my life was a series of contradictions. I exhibited many of the characteristics of poverty, living in a squalid house without hot water, wearing shabby clothes and having open sores on my legs. Yet, we always had servants in our house; even during the worst periods of the war, there was always someone around to help me with daily tasks. I had no mother; yet I was carried constantly as a baby, and received more care and attention than most American children receive. Later on, as my father's wealth grew, we enjoyed some benefits of the upper class lifestyle that I had long coveted. There was death and illness all around me, but new cousins constantly being born. The circle of life and its rhythms are woven into my soul like a Filipino dance.

Although I love my quiet, spacious life with my husband in the United States, I have come to realize the beauty of what I left behind. It is my wish that through this memoir, my daughters, and other Americans along with them, especially children of Filipino immigrants to the United States, will also come to understand at least a small slice of Filipino culture, history, and life, and that my people and my country will be remembered.

Katinka with her daughter Cecilia and grandson Ken

Photographs by Katinka Rodriguez

HITCHING POST ROAD - WINTER 1986

Rodriguez family home in West Lafayette, Indiana

Deck (top) and backyard (bottom) of the family home

Door knocker, Venice, Italy

Arched doorway, Venice, Italy

Plaza, Venice, Italy

Flowers

Boys swimming in Indiana
[Award winning photograph]

Self portrait with camera, c. 1985

Glossary

adobo (Tagalog)
A stew in which the meat is first marinated and then cooked in vinegar, spices, and soy sauce.

Aglipayan (Tagalog)
A member of the Philippine Independent Church (informally called the "Aglipayan Church"). It separated from the Catholic Church in 1902 over the treatment of Filipinos by the Spanish (specifically, by Spanish priests). The church is named for its first Supreme Bishop, Gregorio Aglipay. Today, the church has close ties with the Anglican Communion.

Agnus Dei (Latin)
An invocation, beginning with the words "Lamb of God," forming a set part of the Catholic liturgy.

Aling (Tagalog)
A title of respect for an older woman (the Tagalog equivalent of *Doña* in Spanish).

amah (various languages)
Nanny.

arinolas (Tagalog)
Chamber pots.

Ate (Tagalog)
A title of respect used for an older sister.

azucenas (Tagalog)
White lilies.

bagoong (Tagalog)
A sauce made from fermented fish.

bailarinas (Tagalog)
Female dancers; in this book, specifically dance hall girls.

bakya (Tagalog)

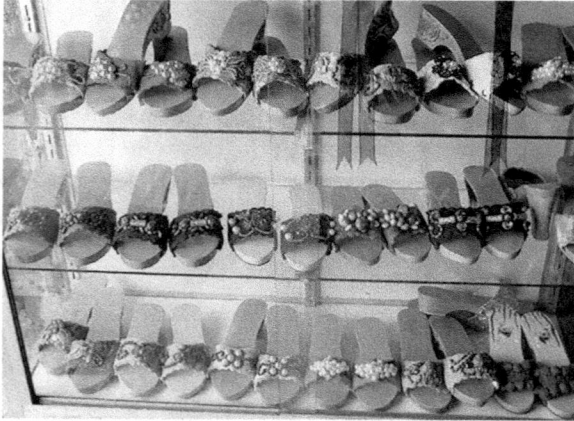

Sandals with thick wooden soles and wide upper straps of fabric, plastic, or rubber that range from plain to elaborately decorated.

balut (Tagalog)
A developing duck embryo cooked in its shell and eaten while still warm.

banca (Tagalog)
A small boat like a canoe.

barong Tagalog (Tagalog)

An embroidered formal shirt for men. Although white is common, they come in a variety of colors.

barrio fiesta (Spanish)
A small town feast.

bibingka (Tagalog)
A cake made from rice.

bino (Tagalog)
Wine.

bumagsag (Tagalog)
To fail or to fall.

buri (Tagalog)
A kind of palm tree.

calesa (Tagalog)

A horse-drawn carriage, often for hire as a form of public transportation.

carabao (Tagalog)

A water buffalo.

carretela (Tagalog)
A horse-drawn wagon.

Cementerio del Norte (Spanish)
The North Cemetery in Manila.

copra (Tagalog)
The dried coconut meat, previously used for fuel, that became a food staple when other food was scarce in WWII.

digestivo (Spanish)
A digestion aid.

dinuguan (Tagalog)
A dish made from animal blood and rice.

El Dia de los Santos Inocentes (Spanish)
December 28, Innocents' Day, a feast day commemorating the massacre of the Holy Innocents by King Herod (he ordered the execution of all male children in an effort to prevent the loss of his throne to the newborn king announced by the Magi).

gumamelas (Tagalog)

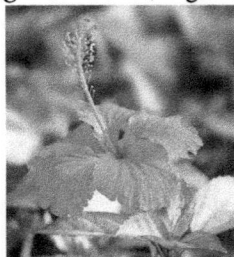

Flowering bushes of hibiscus.

halo-halo (Tagalog)
An ice-cold dessert made of fruits poached in syrup and topped with crushed ice or ice cream.

ilang-ilang (Tagalog)
Fragrant flowers native the Philippines (variant spelling of "ylang-ylang").

Inay (Tagalog)
Mama.

kangkong (Tagalog)

A Filipino vegetable similar to spinach.

kawale (Tagalog)
Filipino wok (shallow and often flat-bottomed).

kokang (Tagalog)
Bartering.

lanzones (Tagalog)

A yellow fruit the size of large grapes that grows in clusters.

leche flan (Spanish)
A baked custard with caramel sauce.

lechon (Tagalog)
Meat from whole suckling pig roasted over charcoal.

longanizas (Tagalog)
Traditionally, pork sausages similar to chorizo (Spanish) or linguiça (Portuguese). In the Philippines, the spices in longanizas

vary significantly by region, ranging from spicy to sweet to sour. Meats other than pork are also common.

lungga (Tagalog)
A shelter; alternately, an animal den.

Mang (Tagalog)
A title of respect used with the first name of a man (similar to "Mister").

media luto (Spanish)
A "medium mourning" period observed in Hispanic culture for one or more years after the first year following a death. It is observed by limiting clothing colors to black and white.

merienda (Tagalog)
A light meal that can be eaten in the late morning or early afternoon (similar to British tea).

nipa (Tagalog)

Thatch; a *nipa* hut is an elevated hut with a roof of thatch.

novenas (Latin)
A form of worship consisting of special prayers or services on nine successive days.

pancit luglog (Tagalog)
A rice noodle dish with a fish sauce, often topped with hard boiled eggs, pork rinds, and scallions. It is a popular street/comfort food in the Philippines. *Pancit* means noodle in Tagalog, but the word is derived from a Chinese expression meaning "convenient food."

patintero (Tagalog)
A street game for two teams of around five players. The field is a rectangle divided once horizontally and twice vertically, yielding six squares (the lines are drawn with chalk). The defending team must stay on the lines, and only one of them is allowed to run along the long horizontal center line. The attacking team starts at one end of the rectangle and must run to the other end and back again without being tagged. The runners use bluffing techniques, distraction, and speed to achieve their goal. For example, one player might draw off defenders to allow another player to get through. The team receives points for each successful run. When a player is tagged, then the teams switch roles. There are many variations to the rules to this popular game.

patis (Tagalog)
A salted fermented fish sauce.

piko (Tagalog)
Hopscotch.

pochero (Tagalog)
A beef dish with potatoes, plantains, and vegetables. It is made from beef stew with tomato-based sauce and saba bananas (a variety native to the Philippines) or plantains, potatoes or sweet potatoes, greens (e.g., bok choy or cabbage), green beans or garbanzos. Other Spanish cultures use pork.

Sabbadista (Spanish)
A Seventh Day Adventist woman.

salakot (Tagalog)

A traditional man's hat with a wide brim and vaguely conical shape. Everyday ones are typically made of rattan or reeds.

sampaguita (Tagalog)

Native fragrant flowers.

santol (Tagalog)

A Philippine fruit vaguely similar to a nectarine.

siniguelas (Tagalog)
A variety of plum.

sipa (Tagalog)
A sport played by kicking an object upward with the foot or knee as many times in succession without missing. Traditionally, a badminton birdie-sized thin paper object in which the paper has been cut up and frilled and weighted by a coin was used. Today, rattan ball or a washer covered in thread, plastic, or cloth is used.

terno (Tagalog)

A native evening dress with butterfly sleeves. In the photographs above, Katinka Floro and her daughter Cecilia Rodriguez wear the same *terno* some 30 years apart.

Tía , *Tío* (Spanish)
Aunt, Uncle.

tinola (Tagalog)
A chicken dish with squash.

zona (Spanish)
Literally "zone"; during World War II, the term became a euphemism for the rounding up and terrorizing ritual perpetrated on the Filipino men within a neighborhood by the Japanese.

Photo Credits

bakya: By Joan Villarante-Kavianifar (Originally posted to Flickr as Mga bakya) [CC BY-SA 2.0 (http://creativecommons.org/licenses/by-sa/2.0)], via Wikimedia Commons.

calesa: By TheHouseKeeper [GFDL (http://www.gnu.org/copyleft/fdl.html) or CC BY 3.0 (http://creativecommons.org/licenses/by/3.0)], via Wikimedia Commons.

sampaguita: "Arabian jasmin, Tunisia 2010" by English: Credits to Habib M'henni /Wikimedia Commons - Own work. Licensed under CC BY-SA 3.0 via Commons https://commons.wikimedia.org/wiki/File:Arabian_jasmin,_Tunisia_2010.jpg#/media/File:Arabian_jasmin,_Tunisia_2010.jpg.

gumamelas: By Muhammad Mahdi Karim (www.micro2macro.net) Facebook Youtube (Own work) [GFDL 1.2 (http://www.gnu.org/licenses/old-licenses/fdl-1.2.html)], via Wikimedia Commons.

santol: By Steve [CC BY-SA 2.0 (http://creativecommons.org/licenses/by-sa/2.0)], via Wikimedia Commons.

lanzones: By Obsidian Soul (Own work) [CC BY-SA 3.0 (http://creativecommons.org/licenses/by-sa/3.0)], via Wikimedia Commons.

barong Tagalog: By Barongguy1 (Own work) [CC BY-SA 3.0 (http://creative-commons.org/licenses/by-sa/3.0) or GFDL (http://www.gnu.org/copyleft/fdl.html)], via Wikimedia Commons

salakot: Photo of a tortoise shell salakot w/ silver decorations in exhibit at Villa Escudero Museum in San Pablo, Laguna, Philippines. Photo by Sulbud. [Modified].

nipa hut: "Stilt house at Kalibo, Aklan, Philippines" by Paolobon140 - Own work. Licensed under CC0 via Commons, https://commons.wikimedia.org/wiki/File:

Stilt_house_at_Kalibo,_Aklan,_Philippines.jpg#/media/File:Stilt_house_at_Kalibo ,_Aklan,_Philippines.jpg.

kangkong: "Ipomoea aquatica" by Eric in SF - Own work. Licensed under GFDL via Commons https://commons.wikimedia.org/wiki/File:Ipomoea_aquatica.jpg #/media/File:Ipomoea_aquatica.jpg.

carabao: "Carabao" by Mike Gonzalez (TheCoffee) - Own work. Licensed under CC BY-SA 3.0 via Commons, https://commons.wikimedia.org/wiki/File:Carabao.jpg #/media/File:Carabao.jpg.

Cementerio del Norte: "Del Norte Cemetery (15164139030)" by SDASM Archives - Del Norte Cemetery. Licensed under No restrictions via Commons https:// commons.wikimedia.org/wiki/File:Del_Norte_Cemetery_(15164139030).jpg#/me dia/File:Del_Norte_Cemetery_(15164139030).jpg.

Quiapo Church: "Quiapo Church Front" Facade by Fmgverzon - Own work. Licensed under CC BY-SA 3.0 via Commons https://commons.wikimedia.org/wiki /File:Quiapo_Church_Front_Facade.jpg#/media/ [modified]

1920 Street map of Manila: "City of Manila, Philippine Islands," John Bach, Philippines Bureau of Commerce and Industry, Carmelo & Bauermann. (Manila: John Bach, 1920). Library of Congress, Geography and Map Division [modified].

Intramuros destruction: By Unknown photographer - Illustration 341 in Medical Dept., U.S. Army: Surgery in World War II: Activities of Surgical Consultants, Vol. II, Office of the Surgeon general, Dept. of the Army, Washington, D.C., 1964., Public Domain, https://commons.wikimedia.org/w/index.php?curid=2696583.

Philippine provinces: By Sanglahi86 - Own work (source file used: File:Ph administrative map blank.png by Scorpion prinz), CC BY-SA 4.0, https://commons.wikimedia.org/w/index.php?curid=47068682 [excerpted].

Japanese invasion of the Philippines 1941: By http://www.army.mil/cmh-pg/brochures/pi/PI.htm, Public Domain, https://commons.wikimedia.org/w/ index.php?curid=2818879 [modified].

SS President Wilson: public domain.

Present day maps: Google maps [annotated].

Philippines on globe: UN Office for the Coordination of Humanitarian Affairs [OCHA] [CC BY 3.0 (http://creativecommons.org/licenses/by/3.0)], via Wikimedia Commons [modified].

Photos of Vic and Paking, Nena at her debut, Tía Emilia and her family, and the Milagros double photo: Courtesy Sharon Floro.

Afterword

On August 4, 2002, at age 66, Katinka Floro Rodriguez passed away after a short illness, leaving her unpublished memoir draft to me, her daughter. Before her death, my mother asked me to edit and seek publication for her memoir. This task could not have been accomplished without the substantial effort and incredible skills of our editor, Æleen Frisch, who shaped a series of recollections and vignettes into a coherent whole while still retaining the author's unique voice. Æleen went above and beyond in all ways to support this labor of love, even designing the cover. Thanks also to my cousins Sharon and Mila Lynne Floro who generously shared photos, family trees, and other information. This book, I believe, reflects my mother's hopes and dreams for everything her memoir might be.

Cecilia Rodriguez Aragon
June 2016

About Alford Marr Press

Alford Marr is a Seattle-based publisher of memoirs
and young adult fiction.

Find print and ebook editions and
sign up to receive notice of new books:
www.alfordmarr.com